Streete...

VALLEYS WEST

Aberaman	4	Mountain Ash	23
Abercynon	26	Nantgarw	38
Aberdare	3	Nelson	27
Aberfan	22	Pentrebach	21
Abertridwr	40	Pontyclun	17
Beddau	33	Pontypridd	32
Bedwas	42	Porth	14
Blaen Clydach	12	Quaker's Yard	27
Caerphilly	41	Rhydyfelin	39
Church Village	34	Senghenydd	40
Cilfynydd	30	Taff's Well	38
Creigiau	36	Talbot Green	35
Cwmaman	5	Tonypandy	11
Efail Isaf	34	Tonyrefail	16
Ferndale	10	Treforest	32
Gilfach Goch	15	Trehafod	29
Godreaman	5	Treharris	27
Hirwaun	1	Treherbert	7
Llanharan	17	Trelewis	27
Llanharry	15	Treorchy	8
Llantrisant	35	Trethomas	43
Llantwit Fardre	34	Troedyrhiw	22
Clwynypia	11	Tylorstown	12
Machen	43	Ynyshir	12
Maerdy	9	Ynysybwl	25
Merthyr Tydfil	19	Ystrad	9

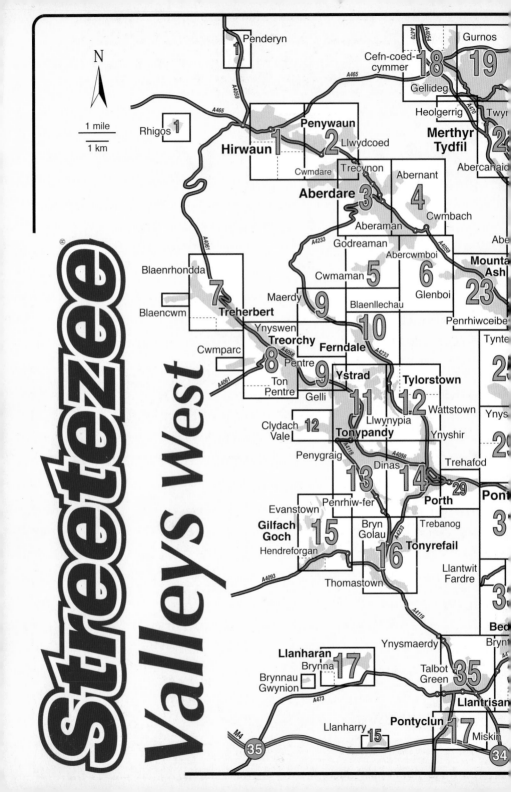

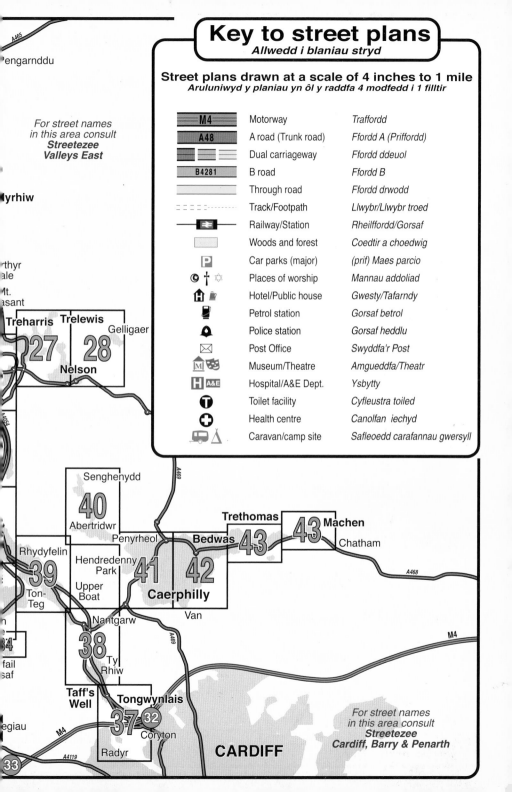

Key to street plans
Allwedd i blaniau stryd

Street plans drawn at a scale of 4 inches to 1 mile
Aruluniwyd y planiau yn ôl y raddfa 4 modfedd i 1 filltir

M4	Motorway	*Traffordd*
A48	A road (Trunk road)	*Ffordd A (Priffordd)*
	Dual carriageway	*Ffordd ddeuol*
B4281	B road	*Ffordd B*
	Through road	*Ffordd drwodd*
	Track/Footpath	*Llwybr/Llwybr troed*
	Railway/Station	*Rheilffordd/Gorsaf*
	Woods and forest	*Coedtir a choedwig*
P	Car parks (major)	*(prif) Maes parcio*
	Places of worship	*Mannau addoliad*
	Hotel/Public house	*Gwesty/Tafarndy*
	Petrol station	*Gorsaf betrol*
	Police station	*Gorsaf heddlu*
	Post Office	*Swyddfa'r Post*
	Museum/Theatre	*Amgueddfa/Theatr*
H A&E	Hospital/A&E Dept.	*Ysbytty*
T	Toilet facility	*Cyfleustra toiled*
	Health centre	*Canolfan iechyd*
	Caravan/camp site	*Safleoedd carafannau gwersyll*

engarnddu

For street names
in this area consult
**Streetezee
Valleys East**

yrhiw

thyr
ale
Mt.
asant

Treharris **Trelewis**
Gelligaer
27 28
Nelson

Senghenydd
40
Abertridwr
Trethomas **Machen**
Penyrheol **Bedwas** 43 43 Chatham
Rhydyfelin Hendredenny
Park 41 42
39 **Caerphilly**
Ton- Upper Van
Teg Boat
Nantgarw
n 38 Ty
Rhiw
fail
saf
**Taff's
Well** **Tongwynlais**
37 32
egiau Coryton
Radyr **CARDIFF**
33

For street names
in this area consult
**Streetezee
Cardiff, Barry & Penarth**

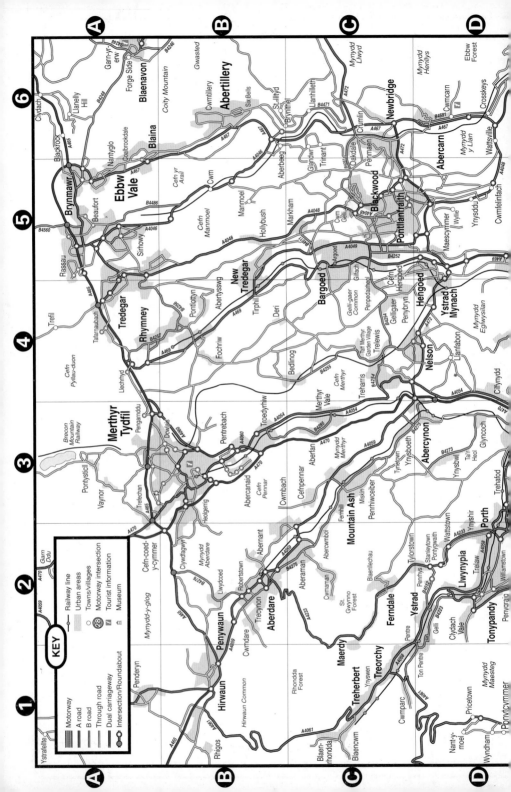

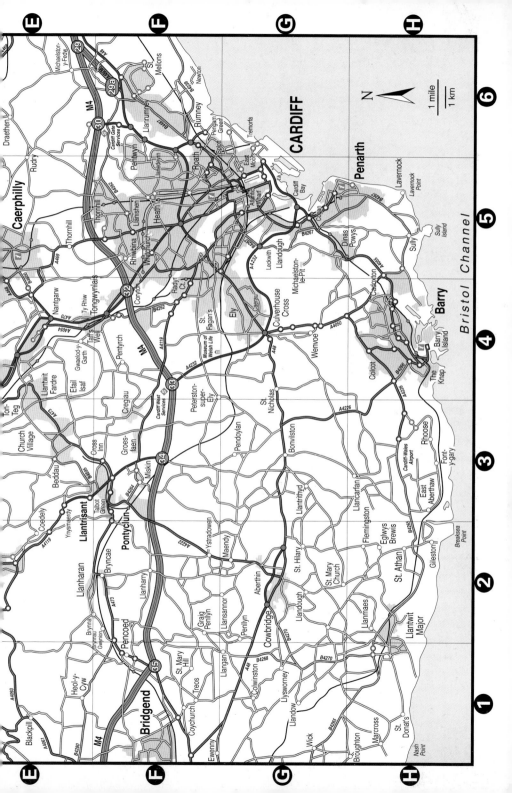

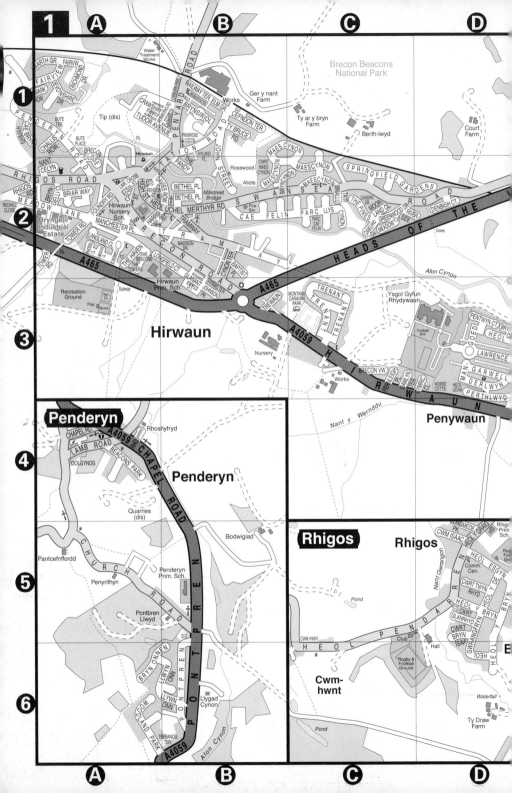

Water Treatment Works

GARTH GR.
FAIRVW.
FAIRVIEW
RICHMOND DR.
MARK
DEVONSHIRE DR.
BUTE TER.
CHALLIS ROW
NANT CELYN
PENDERYN HYFRID
P. CAE BRON
BRECON CLOSE
BUTE PLACE
Fb.

RAILWAY TER. ELM GR.
BRYNSIRIOL
CRAWSHAY ST.
TUDOR AVENUE
PRIMROSE COTTS.
HYLAND
PANDY
UIR CROSS
DAVIES ROW
CROSS ST.
HIGH ST.
KENDON
HARRIS ST.
HEOL UCHEL

CEFNDON TER.
TY BRUCE RD.
JOHN STREET
RAILWARD ROAD
PENYARD ROAD

Works
Ger y nant Farm
Ty ar y bryn Farm
Berth-lwyd
Court Farm

Brecon Beacons National Park

Tip (dis)

Hirwaun

Rosswood
Allots.
MAES CYNON
CWRT MAES CYNON
MAESCYNON
MAESCYNON
BRYNCYNON
S. MAESCYNON
SPRINGFIELD GARDENS
BRAILU
TAIR
OAKBR.
MOORE
LAND CL.
THE PINES
OAKLNG
GREENWOOD DR.
CL. MEADOW
CYNON RIVER
SIDE
DENBIGH CT.

RHIGOS ROAD
RHIGOS RD.
BRYN GELLI CL.
BRIAR WAY
MEADOW LANE
TOWER RD.
LANGLAND CL.
DANWELL
THE HAVEN
THE BEACONS
THE TOWERS
FOUNDRY RD.
Hirwaun Nursery Sch.
MANCHESTER PL.
BETHEL PL.
BETHEL PL.
Millstreet Bridge
MERTHYR RD.
CAE FELIN
PARC LLYS
PARC CAE FELIN
Fire Stn.
MADISON DR.
LONGFIELD CT.
GLAMANT RY.
CINCOM TER.
BAPTIST PL.
PRIMROSE
JOHNSON
SEA
TRAMWAY
TRAMWAY
THE
MERTHYR RD.
M W A Y
HIGH SCHOOL

REDHILL CLOSE
Bryngelli Industrial Estate

HEADS OF THE

A465
Hirwaun Prim. Sch.
Recreation Ground
Pav.
Subway
Tan Cn.
Bowls
A465

Subway
Afon Cynon

FREWAUN
MONTANA CARAVAN PARK
TRENANT
TRENANT
TRENANT
TRENANT
Ysgol Gyfun Rhydywaun
Football Grd.
PENTWYN CTY BRY
GOEDD
HEOL
LAWRENCE
GARWELL
DERLWYN
MAN-
HEOL UCHA
PERTHLWYD
HORSE COTTS.
YMRC
MAN TY
FERN LEIGH
A4059

Hirwaun

Nursery

Works
BRECON VW.

Penywaun

Penderyn

Rhoshyfryd
CHAPEL RD.
A4059
LAMB ROAD
BEACONS PARK
CHAPEL ROAD
DOLGYNOG

Nant y Wernddu

Penderyn

Quarries (dis)
Bodwigiad

Pantcefnffordd
CHURCH ROAD
Penyrithyn
Penderyn Prim. Sch.
Pontbren Llwyd
PONTPREN
BRYN ONNEN
LLWYN ONN
LLWYN ONN
COOMB
TREBANOG TER.
BERM AND PARK
A4059
Llygad Cynon
Aton Cynon

Rhigos

Rhigos
LONGMEDE PK.
CWM ISAAC
HEOL Y GRAIG
Rhigos Comm. Sch.
Comm. Cen.
CWRT TWYN RHYD
HEOL ESGYN
HEOL Y BRYN
CWRT GLANRHYD
CWRT BRYN ISAF
HEOL Y BRYN
GWYNGAEDFRYN
NANT GWRANGON
REN PENDAR
Pond
CWM HWNT
HEOL PENDAR
Club
Hall
Rugby & Football Ground

Cwm-hwnt

Pond
Waterfall
Ty Draw Farm

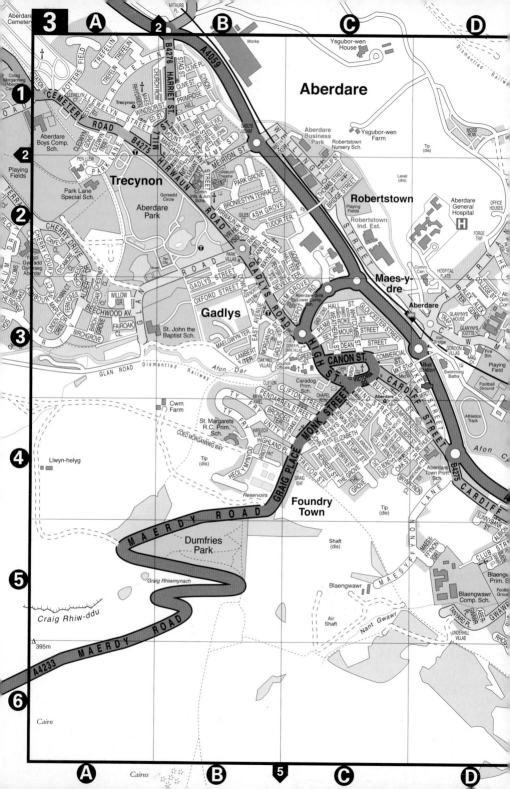

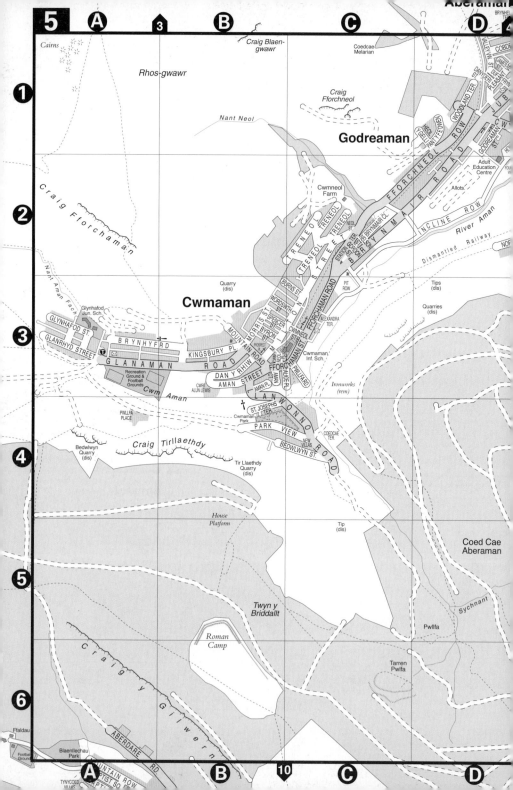

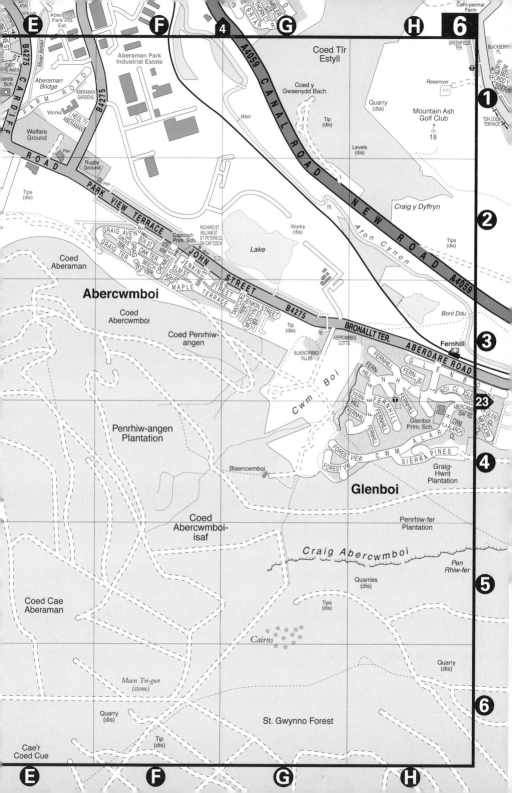

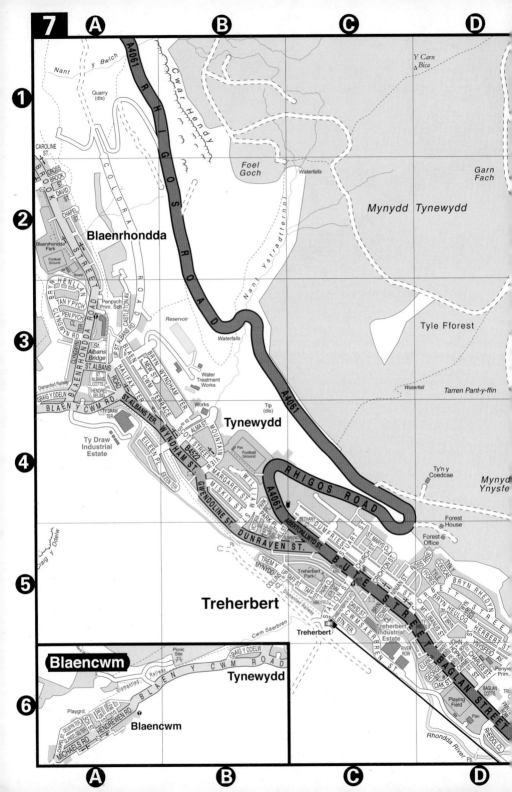

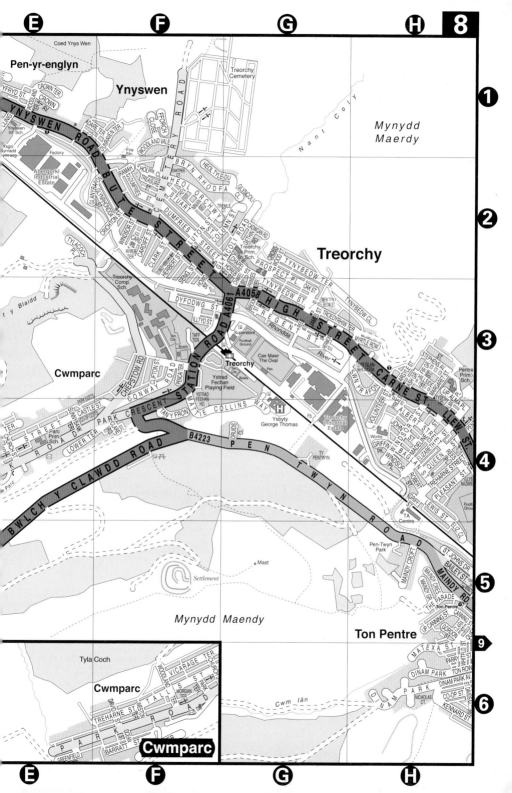

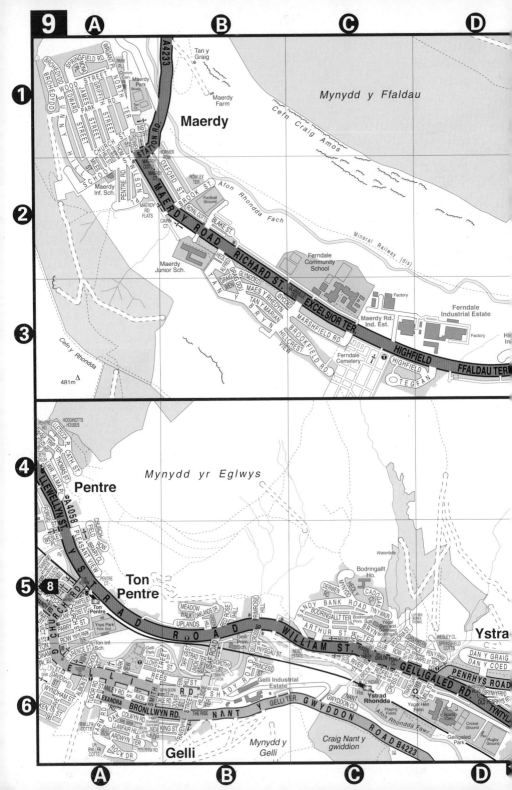

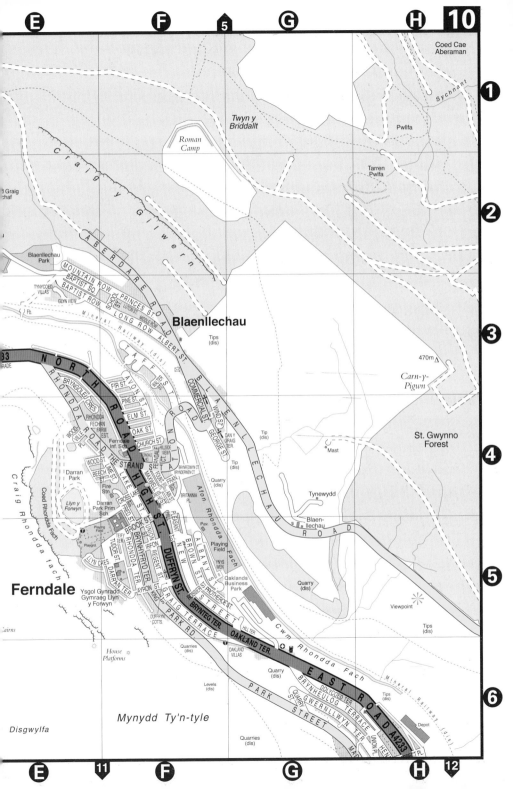

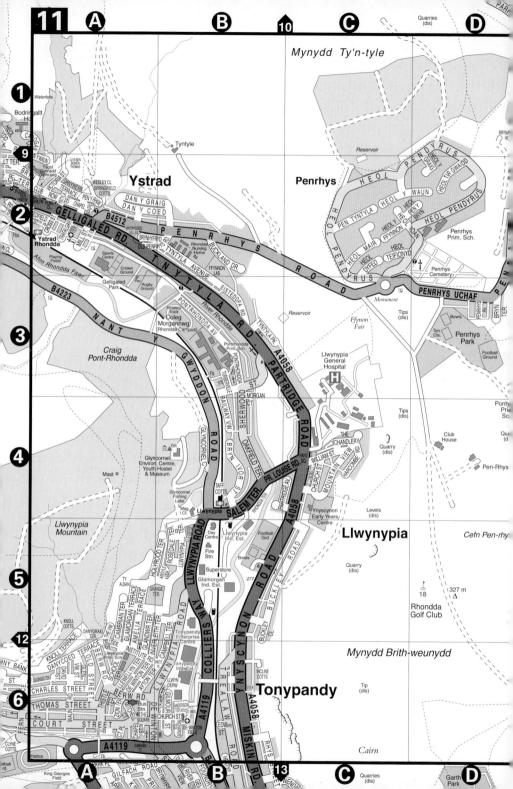

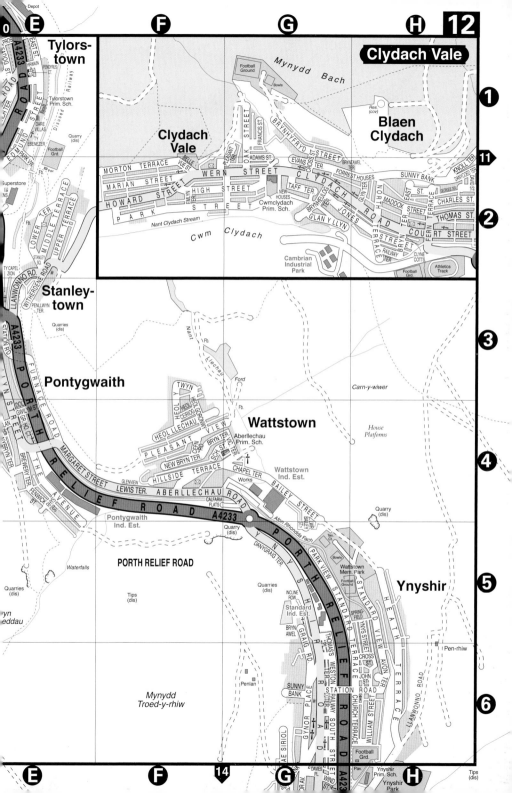

E F G H

Clydach Vale

Depot

Tylors-town

A4233

EAST ST

LLWYNPIA RD

EDMUND ST

DARE VILLAS

EBENEZER

Football Grd.

PARK KWL.

Fb.

Pav.

Quarry (dis)

Tylorstown Prim. Sch.

Superstore

LOWER TER

MIDDLE TERRACE

UPPER TERRACE

STANLEY SQ

TY CAPEL ZION

LLANWONNO RD

WITHERDENE ROAD

PENLLWYN TER.

Stanley-town

Quarries (dis)

A4233

STATION RD

FURNACE ROAD

PORTH

DOL GILW M CDT

GH COTT

Pontygwaith

NYBRYN TER

LLAN

BREWERY TER

THE AVENUE

FENWICK ST

MARGARET STREET

LEWIS TER.

RELIEF ROAD

ABERLLECHAU

GLENVIEW

HILLSIDE TERRACE

CHAPEL TER.

CALFARIA FLATS

Pontygwaith Ind. Est.

Quarry (dis)

PORTH RELIEF ROAD

Waterfalls

Quarries (dis)

Tips (dis)

TWYN

HEOL

HEOL CEIRIOS

HEOL GRONW

PLEASANT

NEW BRYN TER

CEFN RD

BRYN TER

SCH. ST.

Quarries (dis)

INCLINE ROW

Standard Ind. Est.

BRYN AWEL

Penlan

CAE SIROL

GYNOR PLACE

SUNNY BANK

Mynydd Troed-y-rhiw

Mynydd Bach

Football Ground

Bowls

Res. (cov)

Blaen Clydach

Clydach Vale

MORTON TERRACE

MARIAN STREET

HOWARD STREET

PARK

HIGH STREET

BELLE VUE

EILYN TER.

WERN STREET

OAK STREET

LLESANT STREET

FRANCIS ST

ADAMS ST.

EVANS TER.

CROSS ST.

FORREST HOUSES

NEW HOUSES

Cwmclydach Prim. Sch.

TAFF TER.

BRYN MELOG TER

GLAN Y LLYN

BRINHYFRYD STREET

CLYDACH ROAD

JONES STREET

BRYNTAWEL

NORTH TERRACE

RAILWAY TER.

SUNNY BANK

DANYCOED TER

EAST ST.

FERN TERRACE

MADDOX STREET

COURT STREET

CHARLES ST.

THOMAS ST.

GEORGES TER

DAVID ST

BRYN TER

CLYNE COTTS

Nant Clydach Stream

Cwm Clydach

Cambrian Industrial Park

Football Grd.

Athletics Track

Wattstown

Nant Llechau

Fb.

Ford

Fb.

Aberllechau Prim. Sch.

Wattstown Ind. Est.

Works

BAILEY STREET

Carn-y-wiwer

House Platforms

Quarry (dis)

ROAD

PARK VIEW

Afon Rhondda Fach

DANYGRAIG TER

YNYSHIR

STANDARD TERRACE

STANDARD

PORTH

GRAIG RD

YNYS ST

THOMAS ST

WESTON ST

RAILWAY ST

STATION ROAD

SOUTH STREET

CHURCH TERRACE

CROSS ST

JOHN ST

WILLIAM STREET

SPRING FIELD

STREET

HEATH

AVON TER

STANDARD VIEW

LLANWONNO ROAD

HEATH TERRACE

Bowls

Football Ground

Wattstown Mem. Park

Ynyshir

Pen-rhiw

A4233

DRAW

DAVIES PL.

WIND ST

Football Grd.

Pav.

Ynyshir Prim. Sch.

Ynyshir Park

Tips (dis)

1

11

2

3

4

5

6

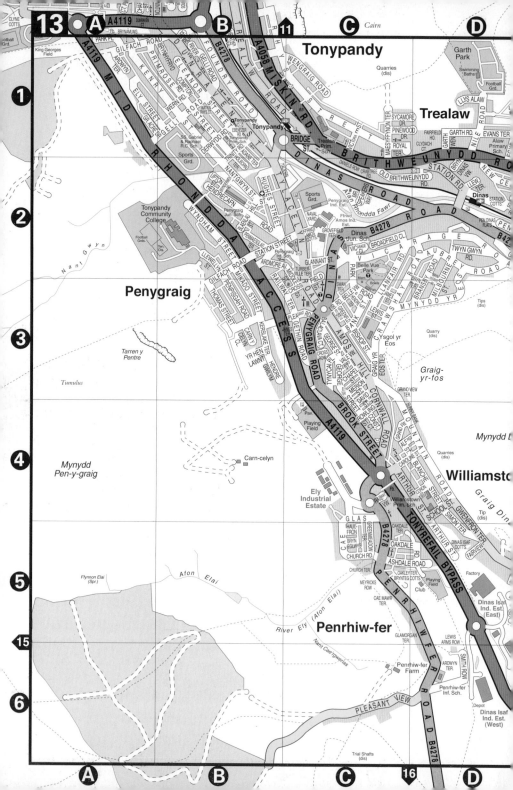

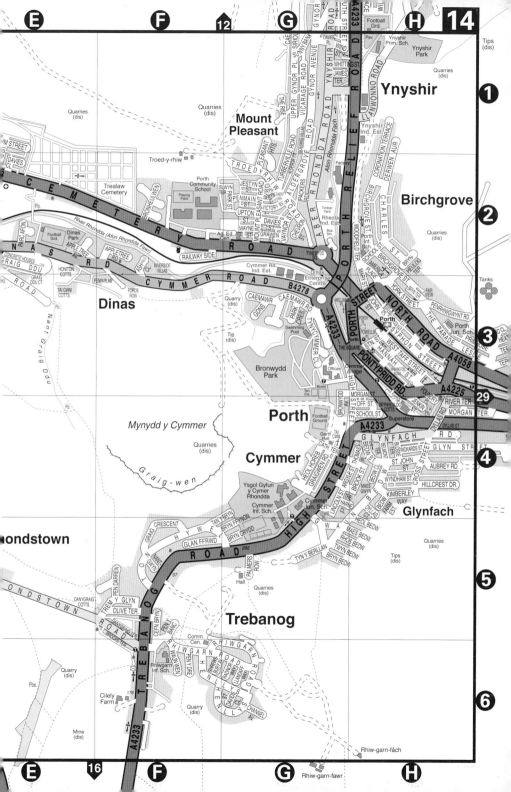

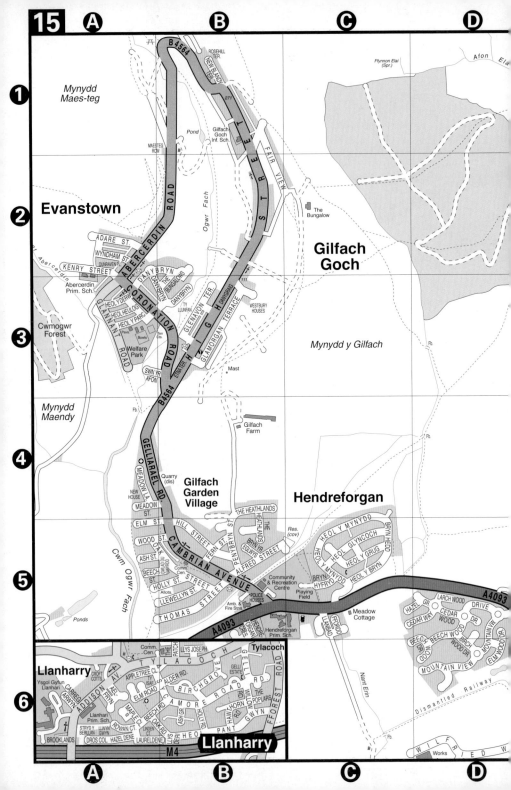

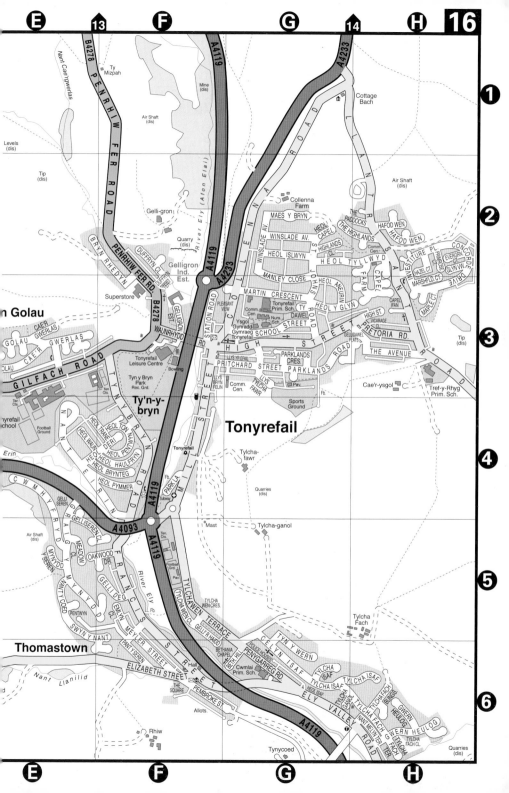

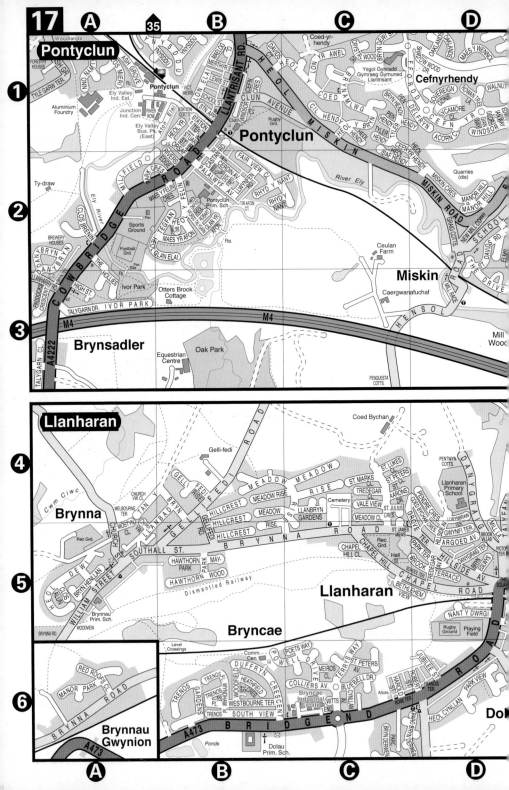

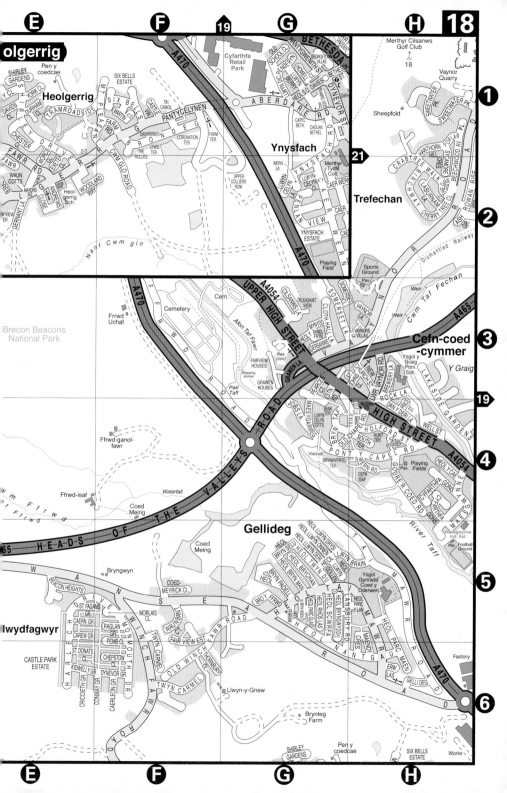

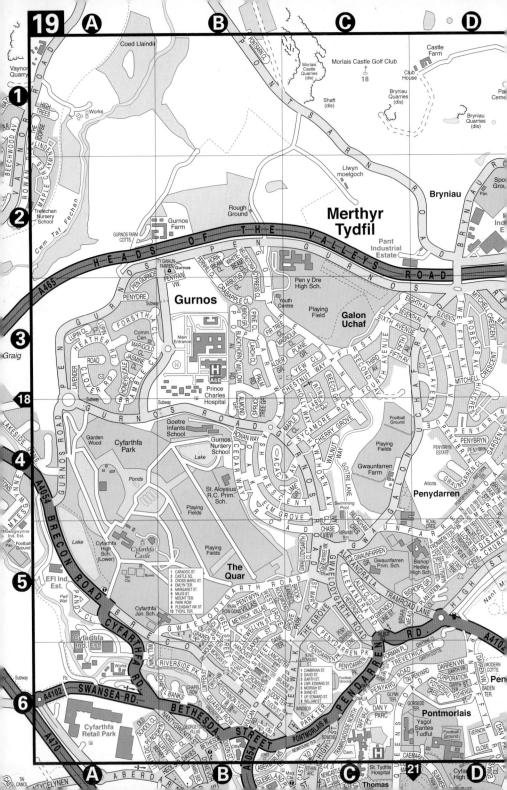

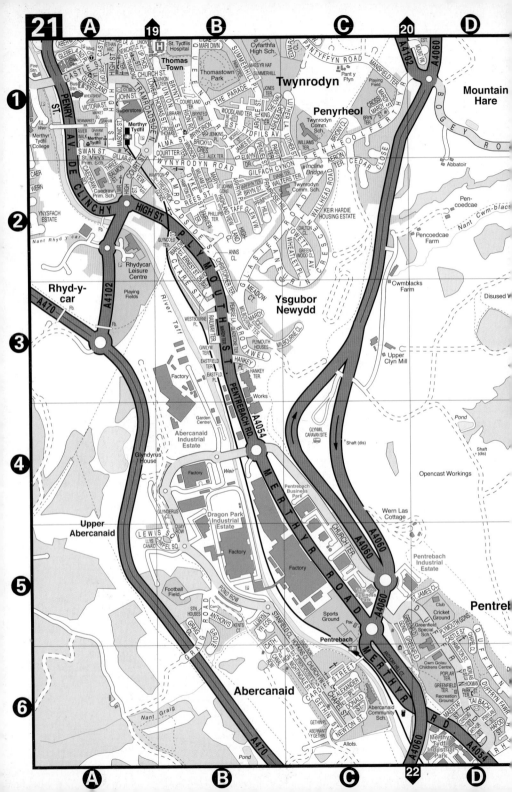

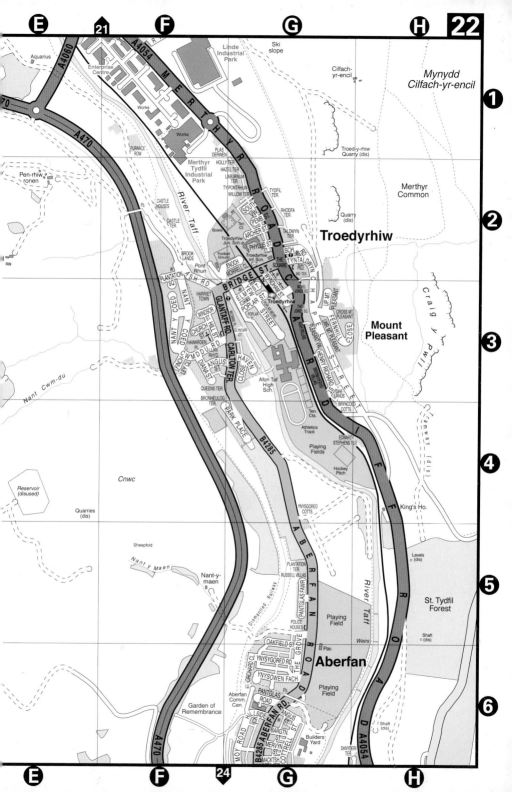

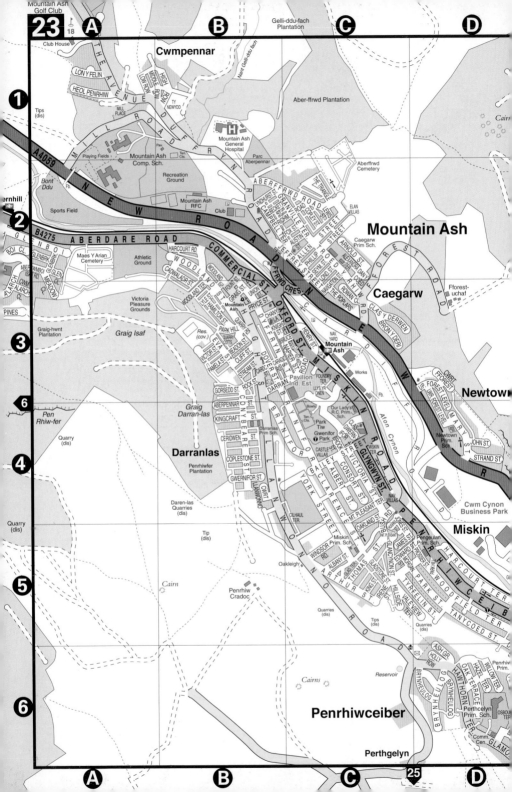

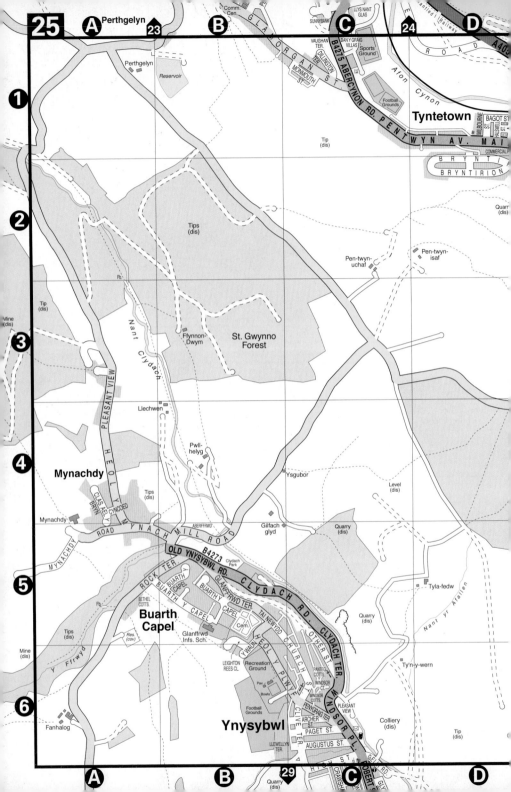

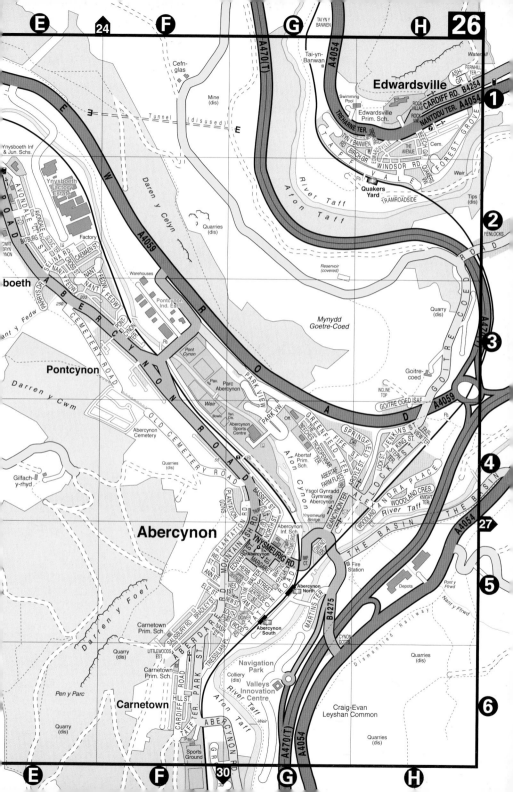

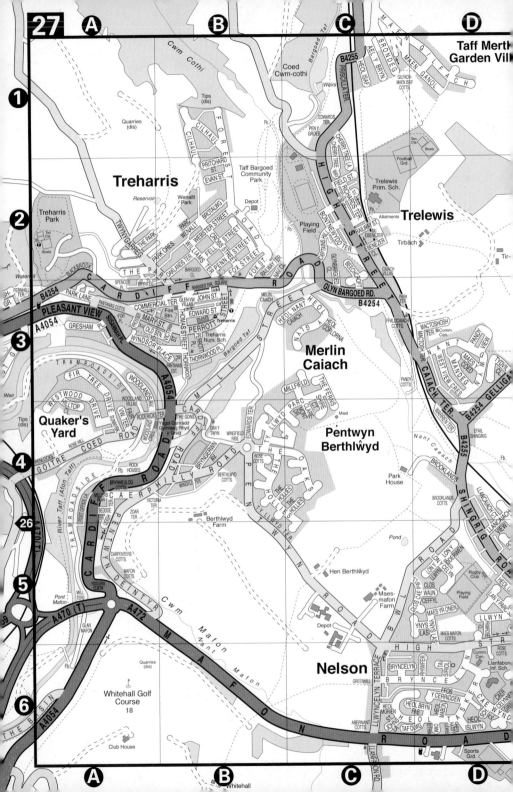

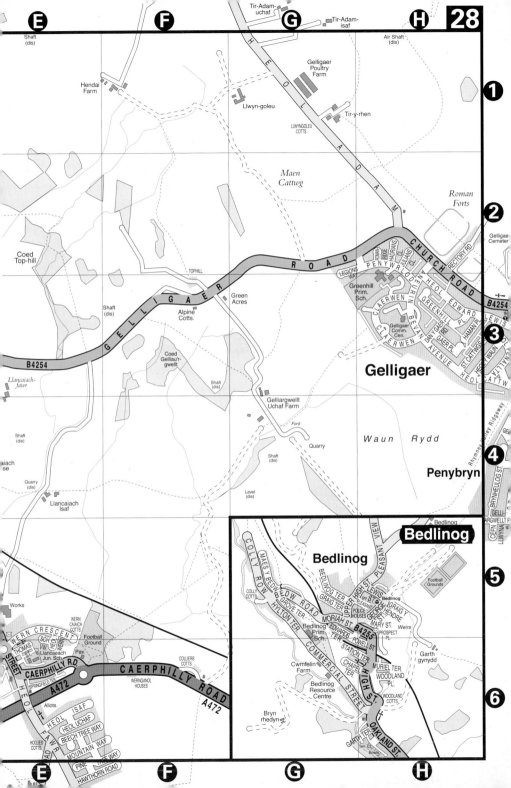

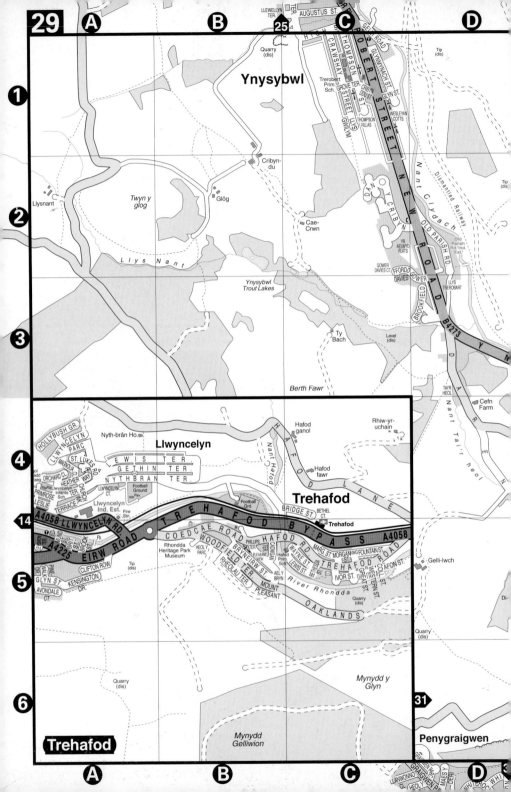

①

Quarry
(dis)

Ynysybwl

LLEWELLYN
TER. AUGUSTUS ST.
HIGH ST.
CRAWSHAY
GROVE TER.
STREET
GWILYM
LLYS
THOMPSON
STREET
Trerobert
Prim. Sch.
CRIB'N
DU ST.
GLYN ST.
OBERT STREET
ROBERT ST.
GLYNMACH ST.
GLYNNYCH ST.
THOMPSON
VILLAS
WESLEYAN
COTTS.

Tip
(dis)

Cribyn-
du

DAN Y CRIBYN
NEW OLD PARISH ROAD
Nant Clydach
Dismantled Railway
Tip
(dis)

Llysnant

②

Twyn y
glog

Glôg

Cae-
Crwn

YR
AELWYD
FLATS

Old
Parish
Rd. Ind.
Est.

L l y s   N a n t

GOWER
DAVIES CT.
FFORDD GOWER
DAVIES
LLYS
TREROBART

③

Ynysybwl
Trout Lakes

Ty
Bach

Level
(dis)

BROOKFIELD
FFORDD GOWER
B4273
Y
N

TA'R
HEOL

Berth Fawr

Nant Tai'r heol
Cefn
Farm

Hafod
ganol

Rhiw-yr-
uchain

HOLLYBUSH GR.
LLWYNCELYN
PARC
ST. LUKES
MAGNOLIA
HEATHER WAY
ORCHARD CL.
PRIMROSE
LESLIE
Nyth-brân Ho.

Llwyncelyn

L E W I S   T E R.
G E T H I N   T E R.
N Y T H B R A N   T E R.

Nant Hafod
HAFOD LANE

Hafod
fawr

④

Llwyncelyn
Infants Sch.
CHURCH
LLWYNCELYN
CT.
Football
Ground
Pav.
Football
Grd.

Trehafod

BRIDGE ST.
BETHEL
CT.

⑭

A4058 LLWYNCELYN RD.
A4225
EIRW ROAD
TREHAFOD ROAD
TREHAFOD BYPASS
A4058
Trehafod

⑤

LLWYNCELYN IND. EST.
Fire
.Stn.
Pb.
CLIFTON ROW
PINE
PINE CT.
WALK
GLYN ST.
KENSINGTON
AVONDALE
CT.
DR.

Tip
(dis)

Rhondda
Heritage Park
Museum

COEDCAE ROAD
WOODFIELD TER.
RHEOLAU TER.
PLEASANT
PHILLIPS
PORTER
HAFOD RD.
BRYNTEG
ST.
HEOL Y
PARC
PLEASANT
MOUNT
AELY
BRYN
Hafod
Prim.
Sch.
WAYNE ST.
LEWIS ST.
IVOR ST.
MARG. ST.
MORGAN
ST.
WG
FOUNTAIN ST.
TREHAFOD ROAD
COLL. ST.
WESTERN ST.
AFON ST.

Gelli-lwch

Di-

River Rhondda
OAKLANDS

Quarry
(dis)

Quarry
(dis)

Quarry
(dis)

**Mynydd y
Glyn**

⑥

31

Penygraigwen

LLANWONNO RD.
GRAIGWEN PL.
MAES Y
DERI
HEOL Y
WHITEHOOK
WHI

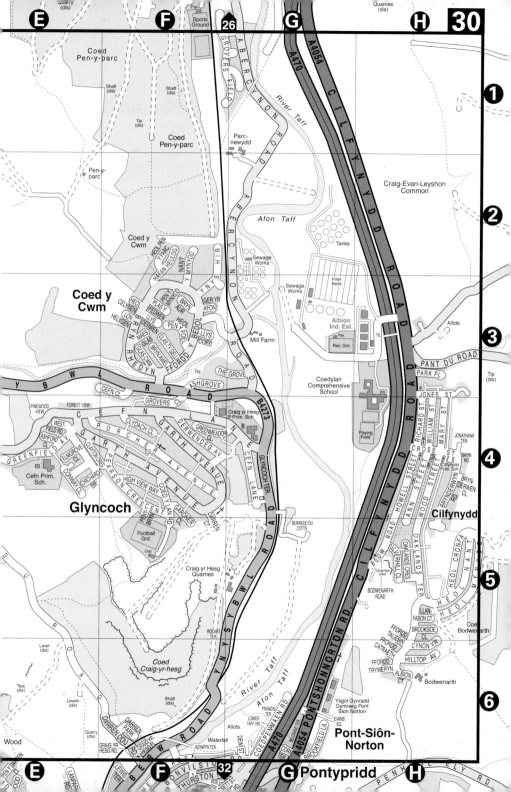

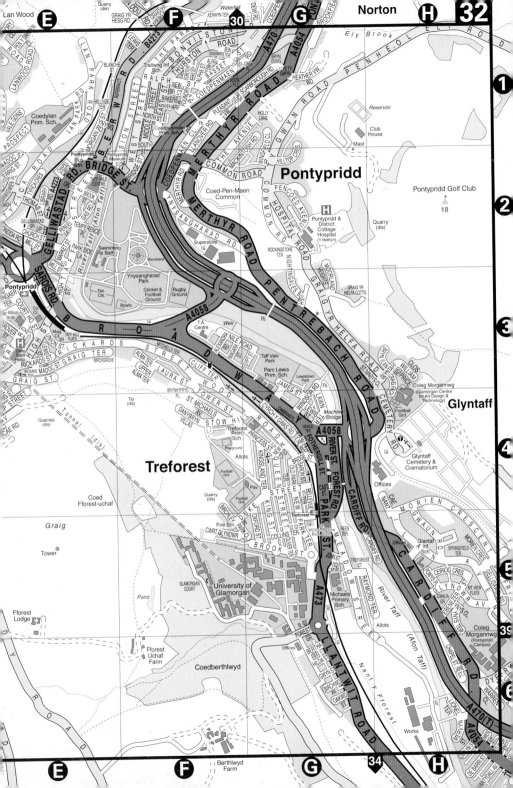

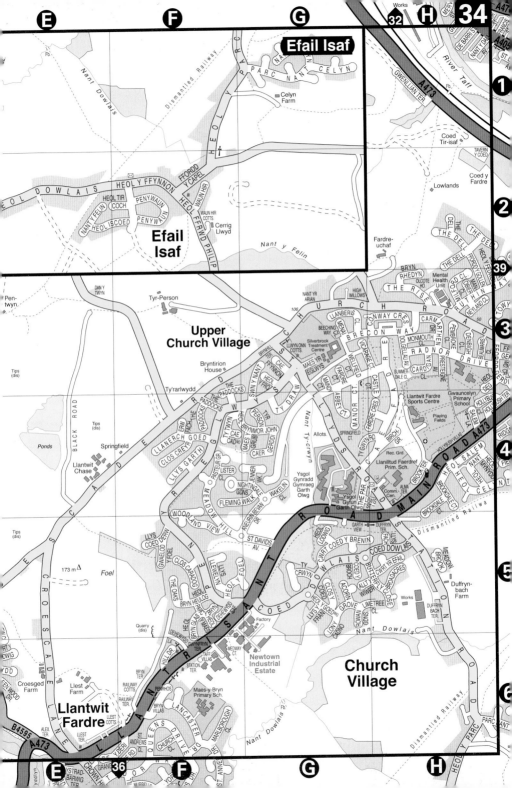

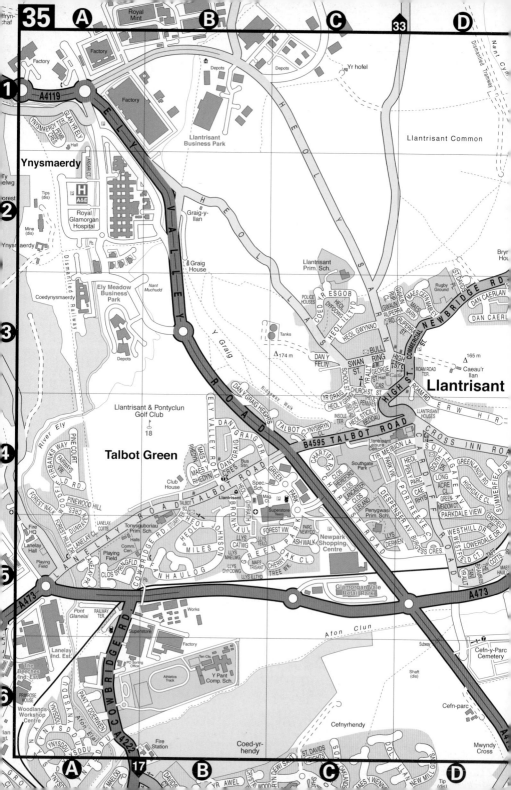

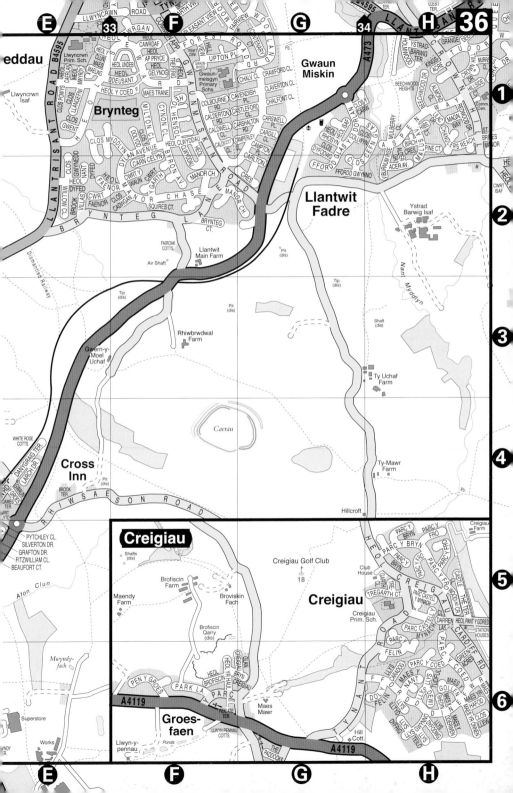

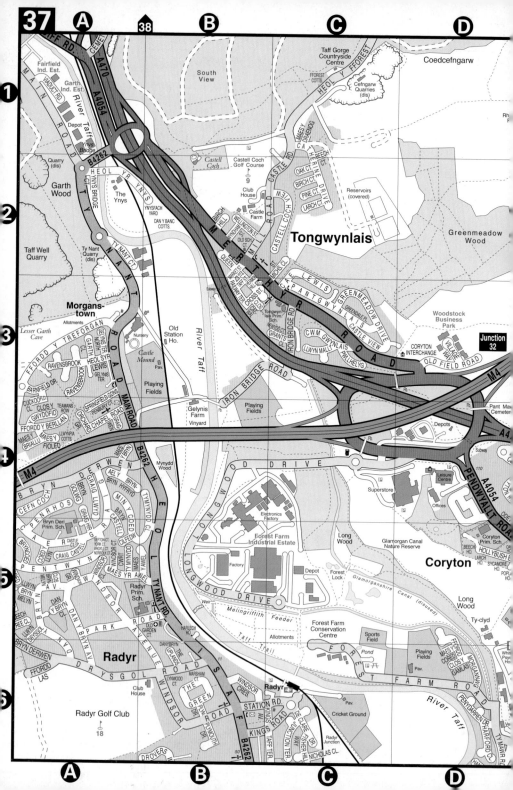

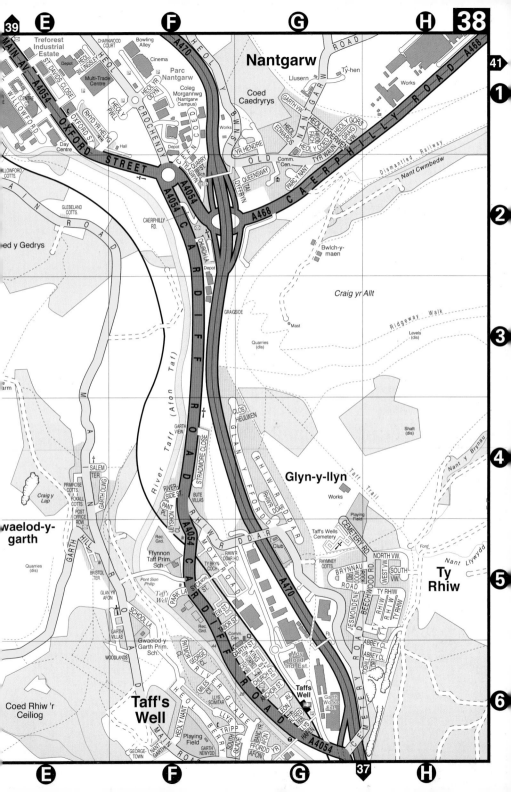

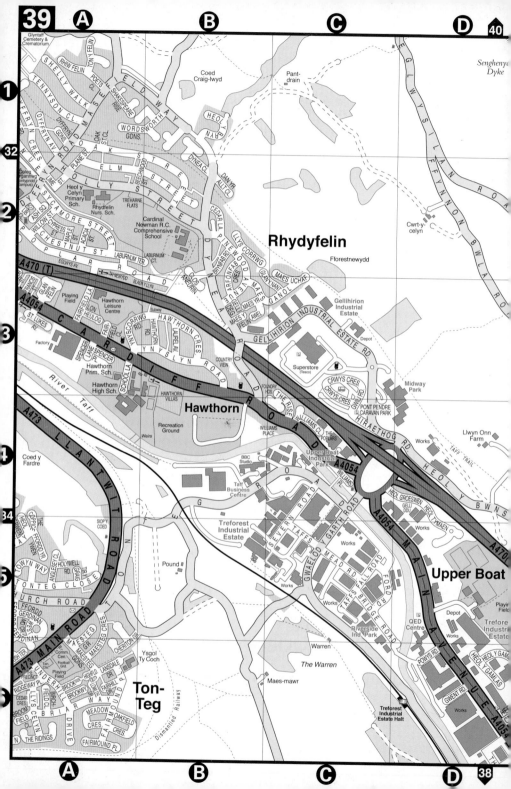

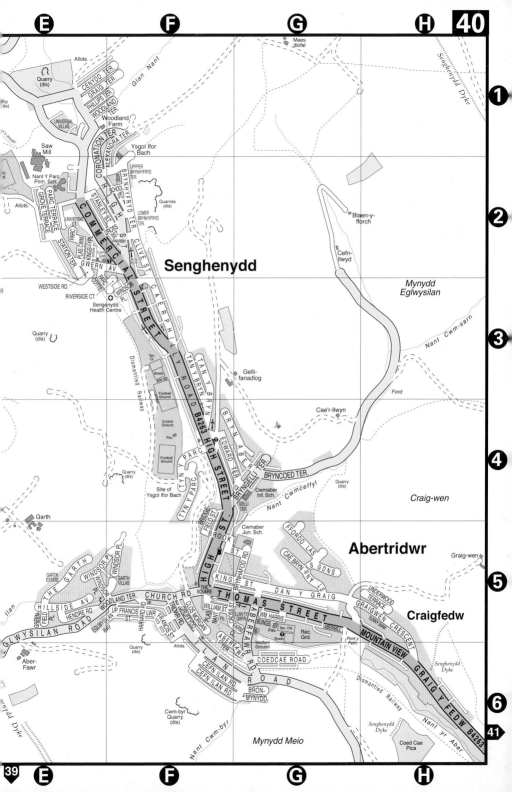

Maes
diofal

Senghenydd Dyke

❶

Allots.

Glan Nant

Quarry
(dis)

Tip
(dis)

CENYDD TER.
GRAIG TER.
PHILLIPS TER.
WOODLAND TER.

Woodland
Farm

UNIVERSAL
VILLAS

CORONATION TER.
ALEXANDRA TER.

Saw
Mill

Ysgol Ifor
Bach

Nant Y Parc
Prim. Sch.

UPPPER
BRYNHYFRYD
TER.

Quarries
(dis)

Blaen-y-
fforch

❷

PARC TERRACE
GROVE TERRACE

STANLEY ST.
SCHOOL ST.
HIGH
CROSS ST.
PARISH

BRYNHYFRYD TER.
CLIVE ST.

LOWER
BRYNHYFRYD
TER.

Cefn-
llwyd

UNIVERSAL

PLAS CWM
KINGS/EPH
PARC

STATION RD.

GWERN

COM
Comm.
Cem.

C O M M E R C I A L   S T R E E T

AV.

Senghenydd

Mynydd
Eglwysilan

WESTSIDE RD.

WINDSOR
PL.

RIVERSIDE CT.

Senghenydd
Health Centre

C A E R P H I L L Y   R O A D

❸

Quarry
(dis)

Dismantled Railway

Ten.
Ct.

Bowls

Football
Ground

TAN Y BRYN

TAN Y BRYN

Gelli-
fanadlog

Cae'r-llwyn

Nant Cwm-sarn

Ford

Cricket
Ground

Pav.

Football
Ground

TYN Y PARC

TYN Y PARC

B4263 HIGH STREET

BRYN ABER

EDWARD TER.

BRYNGELLI TER.

BRYNCOED TER.

❹

Quarry
(dis)

Quarry
(dis)

Site of
Ysgol Ifor Bach

Nant Cwmceffyl

Cwmaber
Inf. Sch.

GELLI
TER.

Quarry
(dis)

Craig-wen

Garth

BRIDGE
FIELD ST.
BROOK
ST.

HIGH
ST.

Cwmaber
Jun. Sch.

FFORDD LAS

CAE BRYN

TAN Y GRAIG
GDNS.

Abertridwr

Graig-wen

❺

GARTH ESTATE
GARTH
VILLAS

WINDSOR PL.
WINDSOR PL.

THE GARTH

CHURCH RD.

BRYNHAFOD CL.

THE
SQUARE

KING ST.
KING ST.

DAN Y GRAIG

T H O M A S   S T R E E T

UNDERWOOD
TERRACE

GRAIGWEN CRESCENT

SUNNYBANK

Craigfedw

HILLSIDE AV.
GREEN FIELD PL.
HENDRE RD.
UP. FRANCIS PL.
EGLWYSILAN WAY

WOODLAND TER.
WINDSOR ST.
HARVARD ST.
LWR. FRANCIS ST.
TEMP. RD.
GLOS MORGAN ST.
GLOS MORGAN ST.

WILLIAM ST.
JESSOP ST.
LLAN TY GWYN

WM. HARRIS
BUNGS.

Ten. Cts.
Bowls

ABERMILL

MOUNTAIN VIEW

E G L W Y S I L A N   R O A D

Aber-
Fawr

Quarry
(dis)

A B E R F A N R D.

L A N

Allots.

Welfare
Ground

Pav.

COEDCAE ROAD

Rec.
Grd.

Pont y
Felin

GRAIG Y FEDW   B4263

Senghenydd
Dyke

Dismantled Railway

Nant yr Aber

❻

CEFN ILAN RD.
CEFN ILAN RD.

R O A D

BRON-
MYNYDD

Senghenydd
Dyke

41

Senghenydd Dyke

Cwm-byr
Quarry
(dis)

Nant Cwm-byr

Mynydd Meio

Coed Cae
Pica

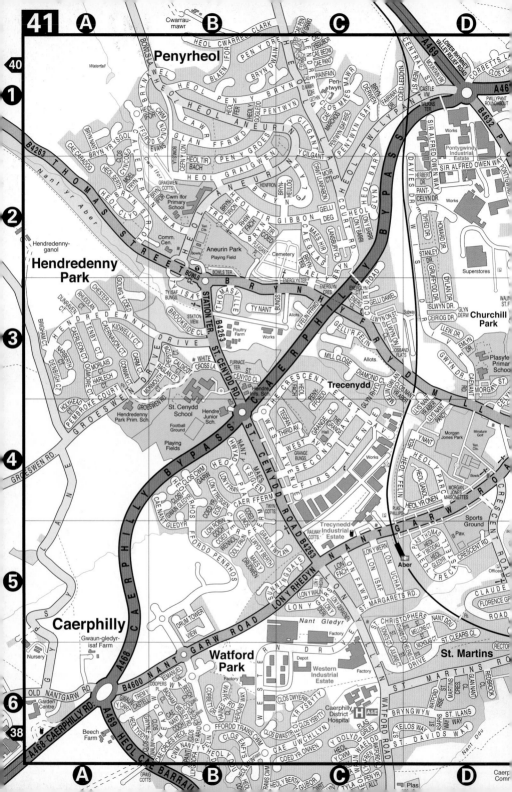

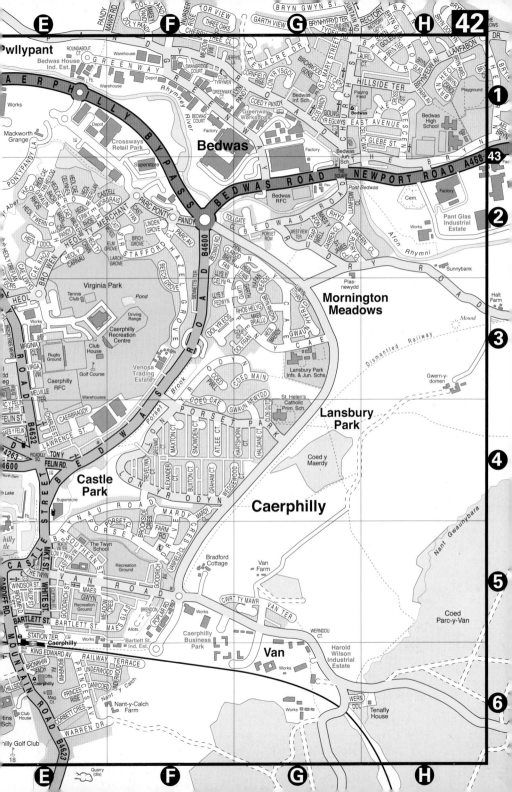

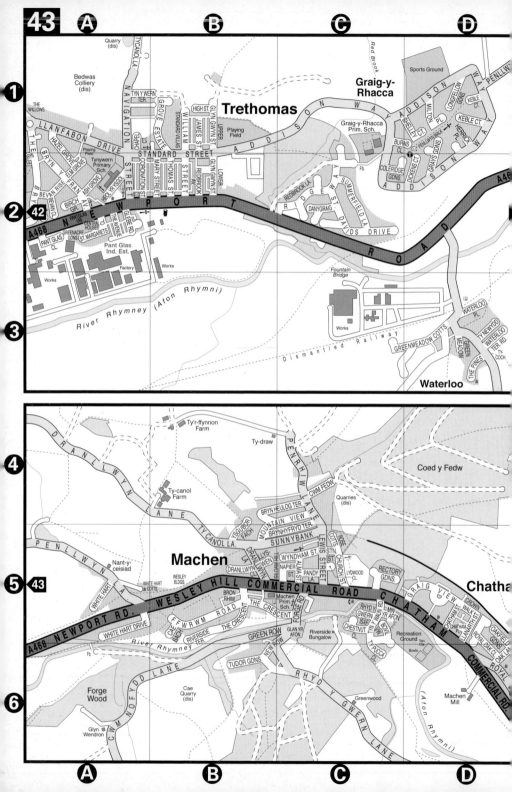

INDEX Abbreviations used

Allot(s).	Allotment(s)	Coll.	College	Fld(s).	Field(s)	Inf.	Infant	Off(s).	Office(s)	S.	South
Amb.	Ambulance	Comm.	Community	Flts.	Flats	Junc.	Junction	Orch(s).	Orchard(s)	Sq.	Square
App.	Approach	Comp.	Comprehensive	Fb(s).	Footbridge(s)	Jun.	Junior	Par.	Parade	Stn.	Station
Arc.	Arcade	Cov.	Covered	Gdns.	Gardens	La.	Lane	Pk.	Park	St.	Street
Av.	Avenue	Crn.	Corner	Gt.	Great	Lib.	Library	Pass.	Passage	Ten.	Tennis
Br.	Bridge	Cott(s).	Cottage(s)	Gra.	Grange	Lit.	Little	Pav.	Pavilion	Ter.	Terrace
Brd.	Broad	Cres.	Crescent	Grn.	Green	Lwr.	Lower	Pl.	Place	Up.	Upper
Bldg(s).	Building(s)	Cft.	Croft	Grd.	Ground	Mkt.	Market	Pr.	Precinct	Vic.	Vicarage
Bung(s).	Bungalow(s)	Ct.	Court	Gr.	Grove	Mag.	Magistrates	Prim.	Primary	Vw.	View
Bus.	Business	Dis.	Disused	Hd.	Head	Mdw(s).	Meadow(s)	Rec.	Recreation	Vlls.	Villas
Cara.	Caravan	Dr.	Drive	Hts.	Heights	Mem.	Memorial	Res.	Reservoir	Wk.	Walk
Cem.	Cemetery	E.	East	Hosp.	Hospital	Mon.	Monument	Resid.	Residential	Wy.	Way
Cen.	Centre	Ent.	Enterprise	Ho.	House	Mt.	Mount	Rd.	Road	W.	West
Cl.	Close	Est.	Estate	Ind.	Industrial	N.	North	Sch.	School	Yd.	Yard

Use of this Index: An alphabetical order is followed.

1. Each street name is followed by a map reference giving a page number and coordinates: Abbey Close 38 H6.
2. Names not appearing on the map are shown with an * and the reference of the nearest adjoining street:
Bagnetts Lane*, Rock La. 18 H3.
3. Where a street name appears more than once the reference is given: Cae Siriol 12 G6/14 G1.
4. There is insufficient space to name all streets in situ, these appear in numbered lists and the reference is given:
David Street (2) Morganstown 19 B6.
5. House numbers along streets are shown: 250.

A

Abbey Close 38 H6
Alexandra Terrace (Llan. Fardre)
.................33 A2/34 E6
Abbey Court 34 G4
Aber Rhondda Road 14 G2
Aberaman Gardens 6 E1
Aberaman Houses...............4 E6
Aberaman Terrace..............6 E1
Abercanaid Industrial Street
.....................21 B4
Abercerdin Road 15 A2
Aberclydach*, Abercynon Road
.....................30 G2
Abercwmboi Cottages.........6 G3
Abercwmboi Isaf Road 6 H4
Abercynon Road (Gilfach Goch)
.................30 G1/G2
Abercynon Road (Mt. Ash) 25 F6
Abercynon Road (Ynysboeth)
.....................26 E2
Aberdare Road (Abercynon)
.....................26 F5
Aberdare Road (Blaenllechau)
.....................10 E2
Aberdare Road (Cwmbach) ..4 F4
Aberdare Road (M. Tydfil)..18 G1
Aberdare Road (Mt. Ash)
.................6 H3/23 A2
Aberfan Crescent 24 G1
Aberfan Fawr......................24 G3
Aberfan Road 22 G5/24 G1
Aberfawr Road 40 G5
Aberfawr Terrace...............40 F5
Aberffrwd 25 B5
Aberffrwd Road 23 B2
Aberffrwd Villas*, Lewis St. 23 C2
Abergwawr Place 3 D5
Abergwawr Street 4 E5
Aberllechau Road 12 F4
Abermill 40 G5
Abermorlais Terrace 21 A1
Abernant Cottages 27 C6
Abernant Gardens*,
St. Johns Lane...........27 C6
Abernant Road 3 D3
Abernant y Gethin 21 C6

Aberpennar Street 23 B4
Abertaf Farm Flats 26 G4
Abertaf Villas*, Glancynon Ter.
.....................26 H4
Abertonllwyd Street 7 C5
Acacia Avenue 19 B4
Acacia Street 39 A2
Acer Avenue 36 H2
Acorn Close 17 D1
Acorn Grove 34 G5
Adams Street 12 G2
Adare Street 15 A2
Adare Terrace (Tonypandy)
.....................13 B1
Adare Terrace (Treorchy) 8 E1
Addison Avenue 15 A6
Addison Way 43 B1/D1
Ael y Bryn (Aberdare) 2 G6
Ael y Bryn (Beddau) 33 C5
Ael y Bryn (Caerphilly).......41 C2
Ael y Bryn (Pontypridd) 31 C1
Ael y Bryn (Radyr) 37 A4
Ael y Bryn (Trehafod) 29 B5
Ael y Bryn (Treherbert) 7 D5
Ael y Bryn (Trelewis) 27 C1
Ael y Bryn (Trethomas) 43 A2
Aelfryn 15 A6
Aeron Terrace 21 C2
Afon Street 29 C5/31 A1
Agents Row 4 E2
Alaw Road.............13 D2/14 E2
Albany Street (Ferndale) ...10 F5
Albany Street (Mt. Ash) 23 C5
Albert Road 32 E3
Albert Street (Aberdare) 3 C4
Albert Street (Blaenllechau) 10 F3
Albert Street (Mt. Ash) 23 C4
Albert Street (Treorchy).......8 H4
Alberta Street 24 H1
Albion Court.......................30 H6
Albion Street (Aberdare) 3 D5
Albion Street (Gelli) 9 A6
Alder Drive 3 A3
Alder Grove (Llan. Fardre) 36 H1
Alder Grove (M. Tydfil) 19 B3
Alder Road.........................15 B6
Aldergrove Court 14 G2
Aldergrove Road 14 G2

Alexander Court.................42 F4
Alexander Place 21 C6
Alexandra Avenue 19 C5
Alexandra Close 19 C5
Alexandra Gardens 3 D3
Alexandra Place 26 H4
Alexandra Road (Gelli) 9 A6
Alexandra Road (M. Tydfil) 19 C5
Alexandra Road (Treforest) 32 F3
Alexandra Terrace (Cwmaman)
.....................5 C3
Alexandra Terrace (M. Tydfil)
.....................21 B1
Alexandra Terrace (Mt. Ash)
.....................23 C2
Alexandra Terrace (Senghenydd)
.....................40 F2
Alfred Street (Gilfach Goch)
.....................15 B5
Alfred Street (M. Tydfil) 19 D4
Alfred Street (Williamstown)
.....................13 C4
Alfred Terrace 38 G6
Alice Place...........................5 C3
Allen Street 23 C2
Allt y Wiwer 34 G5
Alma Place 8 H4
Alma Street (Aberdare) 2 H6/3 B1
Alma Street (Dowlais) 20 E3
Alma Street (Machen) 43 C5
Alma Street (M. Tydfil) 21 B1
Alma Street (Treherbert) 7 B4
Alma Terrace (Church Village)
.....................34 H4
Alma Terrace (Dowlais) 20 E3
Alma Terrace (Treforest) 32 F3
Almond Close 33 A2/36 H1
Almond Grove 19 B4
Alpha House 38 E1
Alpha Place 32 F1
Alpha Street.......................32 F1
Alphonso Street 20 F3
Aman Court 5 B3
Aman Place 5 B3
Aman Street..........................5 B3
Amberton Place*, Merthyr Road
.....................20 E4
Amelia Terrace 11 A5

America Place 14 H2
Amery Place 9 C6
Amos Hill 13 C3
Anchor Street 38 G6
Anderson Terrace 11 B6
Andrews Close 18 E2
Aneurin Bevan Drive 34 G5
Aneurin Bevan Place.........28 H3
Aneurin Crescent 21 B2
Anglesey Close 39 A5
Angus Street (Aberfan) 22 G6
Angus Street (Troedyrhiw)..22 F3
Ann Street (Abercynon)......26 F5
Ann Street (Aberdare) 3 B2
Ann Street (Cilfynydd) 30 H4
Anns Close 21 B2
Ansari Court.......................35 A2
Anthony Hill Court 21 C6
Anthonys Grove 21 B5
Appletree Avenue 14 E1
Appletree Close 15 A6
Appletree Road 14 F2
Arbutus Close 19 B2
Archer Street (Troedyrhiw) 22 G2
Archer Street (Ynysybwl)....25 C6
Ardmore Avenue 13 B2
Ardwyn Terrace (Gelli).........9 A6
Ardwyn Terrace (Penrhiw-fer)
.....................13 D6
Ardwyn Terrace (Tonypandy)
.....................13 A1
Arfonfab Crescent 39 B3
Arfryn (Aberdare) 2 G3
Arfryn (Penywaun)...............1 D4
Arfryn Place.......................21 B5
Arfryn Terrace (M. Tydfil)....21 B2
Arfryn Terrace (Tylorstown)12 E1
Argoed Avenue 17 D5
Argoed Terrace 24 G1
Argyle Street (Abercynon)..26 H4
Argyle Street (M. Tydfil).....21 B1
Argyle Street (Porth) 14 G4
Argyle Street (Treorchy) 8 H3
Argyle Terrace 11 B5
Argyll Court 37 A5
Arnold Street 23 C2
Arnotts Place 3 B4
Arran Close 31 D5

Arthur Street (Mt. Ash).....

Arthur Street (Mt. Ash) **23** C5
Arthur Street (Pentrebach) **21** D6
Arthur Street (Williamstown)
...............................**13** C4/D5
Arthur Street (Ystrad) **9** C5
Arthurs Place.........................**2** H5
Ash Crescent **19** B4
Ash Grove (Church Village)
.......................**17** A1//**35** A6
Ash Grove (M. Tydfil) **18** H2
Ash Grove (Mt. Ash) **23** D6
Ash Grove (Pentre) **8** H3
Ash Grove (Trethomas) **43** A2
Ash Road **22** F2
Ash Square **39** A2
Ash Street (Abercwmboi)...**6** F2
Ash Street (Gilfach Goch) ..**15** A5
Ash Tree Close **37** A5
Ash Villas **22** G3
Ash Walk **35** C5
Ashbourne Court **3** A2
Ashdale Road **13** C5
Ashfield Close **14** F2
Ashford Close **30** E4
Ashgrove (Aberdare) **3** B2
Ashgrove (Edwardsville) ...**26** H1
Ashgrove (Glyncoch) **30** E4
Ashgrove (Llanharry) **15** B6
Ashgrove Terrace (Nelson) **27** D6
Ashlea Drive **21** B1
Ashman Close **41** B6
Aspen Way **33** A2/**36** H1
Attlee Court **42** F4
Aubrey Road (Penygraig) ..**13** D2
Aubrey Road (Porth) **14** H4
Auburn Rise **1** B1
Augusta Street....................**9** A5
Augustus Street................**25** C6
Austin Street **23** C2
Avenue de Clinchy...........**21** A2
Avenue, The (Edwardsville)
....**26** H1
Avenue, The (Mt. Ash).....**23** A1
Avenue, The (Pontygwaith) **12** E4
Avenue, The (Pontypridd) ..**32** F2
Avenue, The (Tonyrefail)...**16** H3
Avenue, The (Trethomas) ..**43** A2
Avon Street.......................**10** F3
Avon Terrace.....................**12** H6
Avondale Court (Abercynon)
....**26** E2
Avondale Court (Porth) **29** A5
Avondale Road **9** A6
Avondale Street................**26** E2
Awelfryn (Pen-y-coedcae)..**33** C1
Awelfryn (Penywaun).........**2** E3
Awelfryn Terrace **19** D4
Ayron Street......................**10** F5
Ayton Terrace **11** A6
Azalea Park......................**20** G4

B

Baden Terrace **19** D6
Badham Close...................**41** B6
Baglan Cottages **7** D6
Baglan Street (Pentre)........**8** H4
Baglan Street (Pontygwaith)
....**12** E4
Baglan Street (Treherbert) ..**7** D6
Bagnetts Lane*, Rock La. ..**18** H3
Bagot Street **25** D1
Bailey Street (Mt. Ash) **23** C4
Bailey Street (Pentre) ..**8** H5/**9** A5

Bailey Street (Wattstown) ..**12** G4
Baili Glas Court*,
    Tramroadside South....**21** B2
Bakers Wharf **32** F1
Balaclava Cottages*,
    Balaclava Road **20** E4
Balaclava Court **13** C3
Balaclava Road **20** E3
Balmoral Close **31** D5
Banc yr Afon **38** G6
Bank Street **13** C3
Bank Terrace **18** G4
Bankes Street **3** C3
Baptist Place **1** B2
Baptist Row **10** E3
Baptist Square **10** E3
Bargoed Close **27** B2
Bargoed Terrace **27** B3
Barnes Street **3** C3
Barnfield Drive **37** A3
Barracks Row **20** F3
Barrett Street **8** F6
Barrington Street **22** G6
Barry Road **31** D2
Bassett Street **42** E5
Bassett Street (Abercynon) **26** G4
Bassett Street (Pontypridd) **32** F1
Battenberg Street **26** E2
Beacon Heights **18** E5
Beacon View*, Alphonso Street
....**20** F3
Beacons Park **1** A4
Beacons, The **1** A2
Beadon Street **23** B3
Beaufort Court **36** E5
Beaumaris Close **34** H3
Beckett Street **23** B2
Beddoe Street **4** E5
Beddoe Terrace **27** A4
Bedford Street **4** E6
Bedlinog Terrace **28** G5
Bedw Close **14** H4
Bedw Farm Estate............**14** H4
Bedw Road (Bedlinog) **28** G5
Bedw Road (Pontypridd) ..**30** H5
Bedw Street **14** H4
Bedwas Court **42** F1
Bedwas Road **42** E4/F2
Bedwlwyn Street **5** C4
Beech Close **41** B6
Beech Court **37** C1
Beech Grove (Caerphilly) ..**42** F2
Beech Grove (M. Tydfil) ...**19** C3
Beech Grove (Treharris) ...**26** H1
Beech House **37** D5
Beech Road **15** A6
Beech Street (Ferndale) **10** E4
Beech Street (Gilfach Goch)
....**15** A5
Beech Terrace (Abercwmboi)
....**6** F2
Beech Terrace Flats*, Beech Ter.
....**6** F2
Beech Tree Close **37** A5
Beech Tree Mews **42** E3
Beech Tree Way **28** E6
Beech Villas*, Graigwen Road
....**31** D2
Beech Wood Drive **15** D5
Beechcroft **27** C2
Beeches, The **26** G4
Beeching Way **34** G3

Beechlea Close **17** D2
Beechwood Avenue (Aberdare)
....**3** A3
Beechwood Avenue (M. Tydfil)
....**18** H2
Beechwood Drive **33** A2/**36** H1
Beechwood Heights **33** A2/**36** H1
Beechwood Road **38** H5
Beechwood Street **39** A2
Belgrave Street **9** A6
Belgrave Terrace **30** G6
Bell Place............................**6** E1
Bell Street **2** H5/**3** B1
Belle View (Penygraig) **13** C3
Belle Vue Street (Aberdare)
....**2** H6/**3** B1
Belle Vue Street (Clydach Vale)
....**12** F2
Bellevue Terrace (Merthyr Vale)
....**24** G1
Bellevue Terrace (Pontypridd)
....**32** G4
Bellevue Villas..................**24** G1
Belle Vue Terrace (Mt. Ash)
....**23** D5
Bells Hill...........................**24** H2
Belmont Terrace (Aberdare) **4** E5
Belmont Terrace (Porth) ...**14** H4
Belvoir Court **35** D5
Bennetts Terrace **42** F3
Berry Square **20** E4
Berth Street **32** G6
Berthlwyd Cottages **27** B4
Berw Road (Pontypridd) ...**32** E2
Berw Road (Tonypandy) ...**11** A6
Berwedd Du Cottages **30** G5
Bethania Chapel **16** F6
Bethania Hill **16** G6
Bethany Court **7** C4
Bethel Cottages **25** A5
Bethel Court **29** C4
Bethel Place **1** B2
Bethel Street **31** D3
Bethesda Court*,
    Llantrisant Road.........**33** B1
Bethesda Street (M. Tydfil) **19** B6
Bethesda Street (Trehafod) **29** C5
Bethlehem View **17** C5
Bethuel Street **3** D4
Bevan Close **43** A2
Bevan Place*, Bethesda Street
....**19** B6
Bevan Rise **43** A2
Billingham Crescent **19** C5
Birch Court **37** C2
Birch Crescent **36** H1
Birch Grove (Caerphilly) ..**42** F2
Birch Grove (Edwardsville) **26** H1
Birch Grove (M. Tydfil)......**19** B3
Birch Grove (Trethomas) ..**43** A2
Birch Hill **37** B2
Birch Wood Drive **15** C6/D6
Birchfield Close **39** A6
Birchgrove (Aberdare) **3** A3
Birchgrove (Church Village)
....**34** H4
Birchgrove (Llanharry) **15** B6
Birchgrove (Pontypridd)....**32** E3
Birchgrove Street...............**14** H2
Birchgrove Villas*,
    Greenfield Terrace **26** G4
Birchley **32** F4
Birchwood Avenue **32** G6

Birchwood Gardens...........**42** G1
Birdsfield Cottages*, Grover St.
....**32** E3
Bishop Street.....................**13** C3
Bishops Grove **19** C5
Black Road **31** D6/**34** E4
Blackberry Place **6** H1
Blackbrook.........................**27** A2
Blackthorn Avenue **19** B3
Blaen Dowlais Street.........**20** G3
Blaen Ifor **41** B1
Blaen Wern **2** F6
Blaen y Coed **37** A5
Blaen y Cwm Road **7** A4/A6
Blaen y Cwm Terrace **7** A3
Blaen y Llyn......................**39** A1
Blaencwmboi Villas **6** G3
Blaengwawr Close...............**3** D5
Blaenllechau Road.............**10** F3
Blaennantygroes Road **4** G4
Blaenrhondda Road............**7** A3
Blake Street........................**9** B2
Blanche Street (Dowlais)....**20** G3
Blanche Street (Pontypridd)
....**32** E1
Blanche Street (Tonypany) **13** D4
Blosse Terrace **14** H4
Bluebell Road **17** C6
Bodalaw **20** F4
Bodringallt Terrace **9** C5
Bodwenarth Road **30** H5
Bogey Road.......................**21** D1
Boi Close............................**6** H3
Bond Street **3** C4
Bontnewydd Terrace **27** C2
Bonvilston Road.................**32** F1
Bonvilston Terrace.............**32** F1
Bovil View **43** C5
Bowens Court **19** C6
Bowls Close......................**41** B2
Bowls Lane.................**41** A1/B1
Bowls Terrace **41** B2
Bracken Rise **4** F4
Bradford Street **42** E5
Bradley Close **19** D6
Bradley Gardens **19** D6
Bradley Street **26** F5
Bramble Close **19** A3
Brambles, The **35** D5
Bransby Road **13** D3
Brecon Close **1** A1
Brecon Place **20** F1
Brecon Rise **20** F1
Brecon Road (Hirwaun).......**1** A2
Brecon Road (M. Tydfil) **19** A4/A5
Brecon Street......................**4** F6
Brecon View **1** C3
Brecon Way.......................**34** G3
Brendon Court **42** F5
Brewery Houses **17** A2
Brewery Lane **18** H3
Brewery Street..................**12** E4
Briar Road **4** G6/H5
Briar Way (Church Village) **39** A6
Briar Way (Hirwaun) **1** A2
Briarmead **19** C5
Brickfield Crescent............**21** B1
Bridge Houses **33** A2/**36** H1
Bridge Road (Cwmbach)....**4** G5
Bridge Road (Upper Boat)..**39** C5
Bridge Street (Aberdare) **3** C2
Bridge Street (Aberfan) **24** G1

Bridge Street (Pontypridd)..32 E2
Bridge Street (Tonypandy) 13 C1
Bridge Street (Treforest) 32 G4
Bridge Street (Trehafod) ...29 C4
Bridge Street (Troedyrhiw) 22 G3
Bridgefield Street 40 F4
Bridgend Road...................17 B6
Brigham Court 41 A3
Bristol Terrace 38 F5
Britannia Place...................10 F4
Britannia Street 29 A5
Brithweunydd Road 13 C1
Bro Dawel 21 B3
Bro y Fan 42 F2
Bro y Ffrwd 18 G5
Broad Street 20 E3
Broadacres 34 H5
Broadfield Close 13 C2
Broadway..........................32 E3
Brocks Terrace 14 F5
Brodawel 2 E3
Brodawel Close 17 B2
Brodeg........................4 G5/G6
Brohedydd 9 A1
Bron Rhiw 43 B5
Bron y Deri 23 C3
Bronallt Terrace...................6 H3
Broncynon Terrace 2 G6
Brondeg (M. Tydfil) 18 F2
Brondeg (Trelewis) 27 C1
Brondeg Street 11 D2
Brondeg Terrace 3 B4
Bronhaul (Cwmbach) 4 G5
Bronhaul (Talbot Grn.).......35 B4
Bronheulog Terrace 22 F3
Broniestyn Terrace (Aberdare)
....3 B2
Broniestyn Terrace (Hirwaun)
....1 B1
Bronllwyn House 9 A6
Bronllwyn Road 9 A6
Bronllys 2 E4
Bronmynydd 40 G6
Bronrhiw Avenue 42 E6
Bronrhiw Fach 42 E6
Bronwydd Avenue 14 G4
Brook Place 9 A4
Brook Street (Aberaman)....4 E5
Brook Street (Abertridwr) ...40 F5
Brook Street (Blaenrhondda)7 A2
Brook Street (Ferndale) 10 F5
Brook Street (Maerdy) 9 B2
Brook Street (Mt. Ash).......23 C4
Brook Street (Porth) 14 H4
Brook Street (Tonypandy) ..13 C4
Brook Street (Treforest) 32 G5
Brook Street (Trehafod) 29 A5
Brook Street (Treorchy).......8 G3
Brook Street (Ystrad)..........9 C6
Brook Terrace (Church Village)
....34 H4
Brook Terrace (Llanharan) 17 D5
Brook Terrace (Llantrisant) 36 E4
Brook Villas (Beddau) 36 E2
Brook Villas (Llanharan) ...17 C5
Brookbank Close 4 F4
Brookdale Court 34 H4
Brookfield 29 D3
Brookfield Lane 30 G6
Brookfield Road 9 C3
Brookfield Terrace*, Merthyr Rd.
....22 G2
Brooklands (Llanharry) 15 A6

Brooklands (Nelson) 27 D4
Brooklands (Troedyrhiw) 22 F2
Brooklands Close 19 C5
Brooklands Cottages 27 D4
Brookside..........................39 A6
Brookside Close (Caerphilly)
....41 B3
Brookside Close (Cilfynydd)
....30 H5
Brookside Crescent 42 F5
Brookway...........................39 A6
Broomfield Close 39 A6
Broomfield Street...............42 E5
Brotalwg............................27 B2
Brown Street 10 F5
Bruce Street 23 C3
Brummell Drive*, Cardiff Road
....36 H6
Brunswick Street 19 B6
Brychan Place 19 B6
Bryn Aber 40 F4
Bryn Aur 30 F3
Bryn Awel (Glyncoch) 30 F3
Bryn Awel (Ynyshir)...........12 G5
Bryn Bedw........................14 G5
Bryn Carwyn 20 E4
Bryn Castell 37 A4
Bryn Close 43 A2
Bryn Coch Terrace.............38 F5
Bryn Creigiau 36 G6
Bryn Crydd 14 G5
Bryn Derw 33 C5
Bryn Derwen (Caerphilly) ..41 C1
Bryn Derwen (Radyr).........37 A4
Bryn Derwen Parc 17 C6
Bryn Dewi Sant 17 C1
Bryn Dinas View 13 D2
Bryn Dolwyn 42 H1
Bryn Eglwys (Llanharan) ...17 D5
Bryn Eglwys (Penrhiw-fer)..13 C5
Bryn Eirw Street................29 B5
Bryn Eithin 2 F6
Bryn Fedw Avenue 42 H1
Bryn Fedwen Close 7 C5
Bryn Ffynnon 14 G5
Bryn Glas 9 A6
Bryn Golau (Tonyrefail) 16 E3
Bryn Goleu (Bedwas) 42 H1
Bryn Golwg 37 A4
Bryn Gwyn Street 42 G1
Bryn Hedd 15 C5
Bryn Henllan (Blaenrhondda)
....7 A3
Bryn Henllan (Brynna) 17 A5
Bryn Heol 42 H1
Bryn Heulog (Treherbert) 7 D5
Bryn Hir 4 H5
Bryn Ifor 41 B2
Bryn Ilan 32 H3
Bryn Ivor Street 11 B4
Bryn Moreia 2 H4
Bryn Nant..........................41 A1
Bryn Olwg 32 G1
Bryn Onnen 1 A6
Bryn Owain 41 B1
Bryn Rhedyn (Caerphilly) ..42 G3
Bryn Rhedyn (Church Village)
....34 H3
Bryn Rhedyn (Glyncoch) ...30 F3
Bryn Rhedyn (Tonyrefail)...16 E2
Bryn Rhedyn (Treherbert) ...7 D5
Bryn Rhodfa........................8 F2
Bryn Rhos 2 E4

Bryn Road 30 H4
Bryn Seion Cottages*,
    Tramroadside South....21 B2
Bryn Seion Court 9 B6
Bryn Seion Street 20 E4
Bryn Siriol 41 A2
Bryn Street........................21 B2
Bryn Terrace (Aberdare) 2 F6
Bryn Terrace (Blaen Clydach)
....12 H2
Bryn Terrace (Llan. Fardre)
.................................33 B1/34 F6
Bryn Terrace (M. Tydfil)......21 C1
Bryn Terrace (Penygraig) ..13 D2
Bryn Terrace (Pontyclun)...17 A1
Bryn Terrace (Porth) 14 H3
Bryn Terrace (Tylorstown)..11 D3
Bryn Terrace (Wattstown) ..12 F4
Bryn Terrace (Ystrad) 9 C5
Bryn Villas (Llan. Fardre)
.................................33 B1/34 F6
Bryn Villas*, Trip Terrace....9 A4
Bryn Wyndham Terrace.......7 A3
Bryn y Fran Avenue............43 A2
Bryn yr Eglwys...................15 B5
Bryn yr Ysgol 41 A1
Bryn, The 42 H2/43 A2
Brynaethnen House...........11 D1
Brynamlwg 13 A1
Brynau Road (Caerphilly) ..42 E5
Brynawel (Aberdare) 3 B3
Brynawel (Bedwas).............42 H1
Brynawel (Caerphilly) 41 A1
Brynawelon 4 H6
Brynbedw Road 12 E1
Bryncanol 42 H1
Bryncelyn..........................27 C6
Bryncoed (Penywaun) 2 E3
Bryncoed (Radyr) 37 A5
Bryncoed Cottages 22 G3
Bryncoed Terrace 40 G4
Bryncynon 1 B2
Brynderwen 2 F6
Brynderwen Close 30 H4
Brynderwen Court 10 F4
Brynderwen Road 13 B2
Brynderwen Villas*,
    Aberdare Road.............23 B2
Brynderwyn Road 30 H4
Brynfab Road.....................39 B2
Brynfedwyn Court 10 F4
Brynffynon Close 3 C4
Bryngelli Close....................1 A2
Bryngelli Terrace 40 G4
Bryngerwn Avenue 27 B4
Brynglas (Caerphilly) 41 B2
Brynglas (Cwmbach)...........4 G5
Brynglas Street 19 D5
Bryngoleu 24 G2/G3
Bryngoleu Crescent 10 E3
Bryngolwg 4 H5
Bryngwilym 9 C6/11 A2
Bryngwyn..........................41 C5
Bryngwyn Close 1 D3
Bryngwyn Street 14 G2
Brynhafod Road 40 G5
Brynhenwyeg.....................31 C1
Brynheulog (Caerphilly)......41 C2
Brynheulog (Mt. Ash).........23 D6
Brynheulog Cottages (Porth)
....14 H4
Brynheulog Cottages (Treharris)
....27 A4

Brynheulog Street (Gelligaer)
....28 H4
Brynheulog Street (M. Tydfil)
....19 D4
Brynheulog Terrace (Aberdare)
....4 E6
Brynheulog Terrace
    (Blaen Clydach)...........12 G2
Brynheulog Terrace (Machen)
....43 B4
Brynheulog Terrace (Porth)14 H2
Brynheulog Terrace (Tylorstown)
....10 G6
Brynhill Terrace 34 G3
Brynhyfryd (Beddau) 33 C6
Brynhyfryd (Caerphilly) 41 B3
Brynhyfryd (Cwmaman).......5 A3
Brynhyfryd (Hendreforgan) 15 C5
Brynhyfryd (Radyr) 37 A4
Brynhyfryd (Tonypandy) 13 B1
Brynhyfryd (Tylorstown) 11 D2
Brynhyfryd (Ystrad) 9 D6/11 A2
Brynhyfryd Avenue 13 D2
Brynhyfryd Place 32 F3
Brynhyfryd Street
    (Blaen Clydach) 12 G1
Brynhyfryd Street (M. Tydfil)
....19 D4
Brynhyfryd Street (Treorchy) 8 E1
Brynhyfryd Terrace (Bedwas)
....42 G1
Brynhyfryd Terrace (Ferndale)
....10 F5
Brynhyfryd Terrace (Machen)
....43 B5
Brynhyfryd Terrace (M. Tydfil)
....18 G4
Brynhyfryd Villas 22 G3
Bryniau Road.....................19 D2
Brynifor 23 B4
Brynllefrith Cottages*,
    Llantrisant Rd. ..33 B2/34 F6
Brynmair 20 F4
Brynmair Close 5 C2
Brynmair Road 5 C2
Brynmair Street 19 D4
Brynmair Terrace*, Merthyr Rd.
....20 E4
Brynna Road (Brynna) ..17A6/B5
Brynnau Road (Cwmdare)...2 F6
Brynnau Road (Taff's Well)38 G5
Brynonen Terrace*, Merthyr Rd.
....19 D4
Brynsiriol 1 B1
Bryntaf (Aberfan).............24 G1
Bryntaf (M. Tydfil) 18 G4
Bryntawel Terrace 12 G2
Brynteg (Bedwas) 42 H1
Brynteg (Caerphilly)...........41 C2
Brynteg (Treharris) 27 A2
Brynteg Cottages 13 C5
Brynteg Court 36 F2
Brynteg Lane 36 E2
Brynteg Terrace (Ferndale) 10 F5
Brynteg Terrace (M. Tydfil) 21 B1
Brynteg Terrace (Merthyr Vale)
....24 H1
Brynteg Terrace (Tonypandy)
....14 E2
Bryntirion (Bedwas) 42 H1
Bryntirion (Caerphilly) 41 B2
Bryntirion (Ynysboeth) 25 D2
Bryntirion Road 21 B1

Bryntirion Street..................20 E3
Bryntirion Villas*, Bryntirion Rd.
....21 B1
Brynwern Street..................20 F2
Brynygwaith Villlas*, Bryn Moreia
....2 H4
Bryony Close......................21 C1
Buarth Glas Terrace 24 H6
Buarth y Capel...................25 B5
Buckland Drive 11 B2
Buckley Close 11 B5
Buckley Road 11 B5
Bull Ring 35 C3
Bungalows, The.................15 B3
Burgess Crescent 35 D5
Burns Close 43 C1
Burns Street 5 C3
Burns Way 31 D5
Bush Road...........................23 C5
Bute Cottages 17 B1
Bute Place 1 A1
Bute Square 7 C5
Bute Street (Aberdare) 3 C3
Bute Street (Treherbert) 7 C5
Bute Street (Treorchy)..........8 F2
Bute Terrace (Aberdare) 3 D4
Bute Terrace (Hirwaun) 1 A1
Bute Villas 38 F4
Butterfly Close....................34 G5
Buxton Court 42 F4
Bwl Road 27 C5
Bwlch y Clawdd Road 8 E5
Bwllfa Cottages 9 A6
Bwllfa Dare Terrace*, Bwllfa Rd.
....2 E6
Bwllfa Road 2 E6
Bwllfa Row*, Bwllfa Road 2 E6
Byron Avenue 36 F2
Byron Street..........................5 B3

C

Cadlan Bethel 18 G1
Cadogan Close 9 C5/11 A1
Cadwaladr Street...............23 B2
Cadwgan Road 8 G2
Cadwgan Terrace 29 B5
Cae Bach 43 B5
Cae Bedw 41 C1
Cae Bryn 40 G5
Cae Bryn Hyfryd 1 A1
Cae Cadno..........................34 F4
Cae Calch 41 C1
Cae Caradog 41 A1
Cae Croes Heol 41 B6
Cae Du Mawr 41 C1
Cae Fadre 34 H4
Cae Felin Parc......................1 B2
Cae Ffynnon (Caerphilly) ...41 C1
Cae Ffynnon (Church Village)
....34 G3
Cae Gethin..........................41 C1
Cae Glas (Penrhiw-fer) 13 C5
Cae Lewis 37 C3
Cae Llwyd 42 E2
Cae Marchog.......................41 C1
Cae Mari Dwn 21 B1
Cae Mawr Terrace..............13 C5
Cae Nant 32 H4
Cae Nant Coch 41 B6
Cae Nant Gledyr 41 B4
Cae Pandy...........................42 E2
Cae Pant 41 C1
Cae Pen y Graig 41 C1

Cae Rhos............................42 E2
Cae Rhys.............................35 D4
Cae Siriol 12 G6/14 G1
Cae Uwchllyn 41 C6
Cae Wyndu 27 D6
Cae Ysgubor 41 C1
Cae'r Gerddi 34 G4
Cae'r Gwerlas 16 E3
Caeglas (Caerphilly) 41 C2
Caemaen Street 26 E2
Caemawr Gardens 14 G3
Caemawr Road 14 G3
Caenant Road 41 D3
Caer Celynnen 27 D6
Caer Fferm 41 B4
Caer Graig 37 A5
Caer Wern 18 G2/21 A2
Caeracca Farm Estate 20 G1
Caeracca Villas............20 F1/F2
Caerbragdy 42 E4
Caerdraw Road 21 A2
Caerhendy Street 20 E4
Caerleon Court 41 A3
Caerleon Grove 18 F6
Caernarvon Court 41 A3
Caernarvon Grove 18 E5
Caerphilly Bypass ...41 A5/42 E1
Caerphilly Road (Caerphilly)
....41 A6
Caerphilly Road (Nantgarw)
....38 F2/G2
Caerphilly Road (Nelson)
....28 E6/F6
Caerphilly Road (Senghenydd)
....40 F3
Caerphilly Road (Treharris) 27 A4
Caiach Terrace 27 D3
Caiach Villas 27 C2
Cairn Court 9 B2
Cairo Street 14 E2
Calderton Road 36 F1
Caldicot Court 41 B3
Caldicott Close....................36 F1
Caldwell Close 36 F2
Caledfryn Way 41 A1
Calfaria Flats 12 F4
Calluna Close 20 G4
Cambrian Avenue 15 B5
Cambrian Place...................32 G4
Cambrian Street (1)............19 C5
Cambrian Terrace (M. Tydfil)
....19 C5
Cambrian Terrace (Tonypandy)
....11 A5
Camellia Close 2 G6/3 A2
Campbell Terrace (Mt. Ash)
....23 B2
Campbell Terrace (Tonypandy)
....11 A6
Camperly Close..................36 G1
Campton Place 36 G1
Canal Cottages*,
          Coedpenmaen Rd. ...32 F1
Canal Lock Close 24 G3
Canal Road 4 F4/G6/6 G1
Canal Row 21 B6
Canning Street 8 H5
Canon Street 3 C3
Canonbie Crescent 24 G2
Capel Bethlehem................18 G1
Capel Farm 16 H2
Capel Ifan 16 H3
Captains Hill 27 C2

Caradoc Road 23 B3
Caradoc Street (1) (M. Tydfil)
....19 B5
Caradoc Street (Mt. Ash)...23 B3
Caradog Road 11 D1
Cardiff Place 8 F2
Cardiff Road (Abercynon) ..26 F6
Cardiff Road (Aberdare)
..........................3 D4/4 E5/6 E1
Cardiff Road (Caerphilly) ...42 E5
Cardiff Road (Creigiau) 36 H5
Cardiff Road (Edwardsville)26 H1
Cardiff Road (Hawthorn) 39 A3
Cardiff Road (Llantrisant) ..35 D4
Cardiff Road (Merthyr Vale)
....24 H1
Cardiff Road (Mt. Ash)........23 C3
Cardiff Road (Quaker's Yard)
....27 A5
Cardiff Road (Rhydyfelin) ..32 H6
Cardiff Road (Taff's Well) ..38 F2
Cardiff Road (Treforest)
......................................32 G4/G5/H5
Cardiff Road (Treharris) 27A3
Cardiff Road (Troedyrhiw)..22 G3
Cardiff Street (Abercanaid) 21 C6
Cardiff Street (Aberdare) 3 C3
Cardiff Street (Treorchy) 8 F2
Cardigan Close 34 H3
Carew Grove 18 E5
Cargill Close 36 G1
Carlton Crescent 36 G2
Carlton Terrace 22 G3
Carmarthen Court 41 A3
Carmarthen Drive 34 H3
Carmel Street 7 D6
Carn Celyn..........................36 F2
Carn y Celyn Close 13 B3
Carne Street 8 H3
Caroline Street (Blaenrhondda)
....7 A1
Caroline Street (Williamstown)
....13 C4
Carpenters Cottages 27 A5
Carreg Arwyn 15 A6
Carshalton Road 36 G1
Carswell Place 36 G1
Cascade View 2 F6
Castan Road 17 B2
Castell Meredydd...............42 F2
Castell Morgraig 42 E2
Castell y Fan 42 F2
Castell y Mynach 33 C6
Castellau Road 33 A5
Castle Close 36 H5
Castle Coch View 37 C2
Castle Court (Church Village)
....34 H3
Castle Court (Radyr) 37 A5
Castle Houses 22 B2
Castle Ifor Street 31 D2
Castle Park Estate 18 E6
Castle Road.........................37 C2
Castle Row 20 G2
Castle Square (2) 19 B5
Castle Street (Caerphilly) ..42 E5
Castle Street (Llantrisant) .35 C3
Castle Street (M. Tydfil) 21 A1
Castle Street (Pentrebach) 15 B5
Castle Street (Taff's Well) .38 G6
Castle Street (Treforest) 32 G4
Castle Street (Treorchy) 8 E4
Castle Terrace 22 F2

Castle View (Caerphilly) 41 D1
Castle View (M. Tydfil).......18 F2
Castle View (Tongwynlais) 37 C3
Castle Villas........................23 C4
Castle Yard 21 A1
Castleford Close 36 G1
Castleton Avenue 7 A2
Caswell Close 1 A2
Catherine Close..................21 B6
Catherine Drive 37 C1
Catherine Street (Aberdare) 3 C4
Catherine Street (Pentre) 9 A4
Catherine Terrace 14 G4
Catherines Court*,
      Tramroadside South....21 B2
Cavendish Place.................36 G1
Cedar Close (Aberdare) 3 A3
Cedar Close (M. Tydil) 21 C2
Cedar Crescent 39 A6
Cedar Lane 39 B2
Cedar Way (Hendreforgan) 15 C5
Cedar Way (Merthyr Tydil) 19 B4
Cedar Wood Drive 15 D5
Cefn Bryn 14 F5
Cefn Close 30 F3
Cefn Coch 37 A4
Cefn Coed 38 F2
Cefn Isaf 18 H4
Cefn Lane 30 E4/G4
Cefn Llan Road 40 F6
Cefn Llwyna.........................28 H5
Cefn Pennar Cottages*,
      The Avenue 23 A1
Cefn Road 12 F4
Cefn y Lon 41 B2
Cefndon Terrace 1 B1
Cefnpennar Road 4 G5/H1
Ceiriog Crescent 32 H5
Ceiriog Drive 41 D3
Celtic Way 42 H1
Celyn Avenue 41 D4
Celyn Grove 41 D4
Celyn Isaf 16 G6
Cemetery Road (Abercynon)
....26 E3
Cemetery Road (Aberdare)
....2 G5/3 A1
Cemetery Road (Porth) 14 G2
Cemetery Road (Taff's Well)
....37 A1/38 G6
Cemetery Road (Treforest) 32 H4
Cemetery Road (Treorchy) ..8 F2
Cenarth Drive 4 G3
Centenary Court 33 D6
Central Houses 43 A2
Central Square*, Ralph St. 32 F1
Central Street 41 D1
Centre Court 38 E1
Cenydd Terrace 40 E1
Cerdin Avenue 17 B2
Cerdinen Terrace 4 G5
Ceredig Street 21 D6
Ceridwen Street (Maerdy) ...9 A1
Ceridwen Street (Mt. Ash) .23 B4
Ceridwen Terrace*,
      Heol y Beiliau 35 C4
Chalfont Close 36 G1
Challis Row 1 A1
Chalvington Close 36 G1
Chancery Lane 23 B3
Chandlers Reach 36 H1
Chandlery, The 11 C4
Channel Avenue 14 G6

Chapel Banks **19** A6
Chapel Close......................**21** D5
Chapel Court **43** A1
Chapel Hill **17** C5
Chapel Hill Close...............**17** C5
Chapel Road (Llanharan) ..**17** D5
Chapel Road (Penderyn)......**1** A4
Chapel Road (Radyr)..........**37** A4
Chapel Row (Aberdare)........**3** C3
Chapel Row (M. Tydfil) **19** B6
Chapel Square...................**21** B5
Chapel Street (Abercanaid)**21** C5
Chapel Street (Aberdare) **4** E6
Chapel Street (Blaencwm)....**7** A6
Chapel Street (Blaenrhondda)
....**7** A2
Chapel Street (Pentre).........**9** A5
Chapel Street (Penygraig)..**13** C3
Chapel Street (Pontypridd) **32** E2
Chapel Street (Rhydyfelin) **32** H6
Chapel Street (Tonypandy) **11** A6
Chapel Street (Treorchy)......**8** G3
Chapel Street (Troedyrhiw) **22** G3
Chapel Street (Ystrad)
.............................**9** D6/**11** A2
Chapel Terrace (Bedlinog) **28** G6
Chapel Terrace (Wattstown)
....**12** G4
Charles Street (Caerphilly) **42** E4
Charles Street (Pontypridd) **31** D2
Charles Street (Porth) **14** H2
Charles Street (Tonypandy)
..............................**11** A6/**12** H2
Charles Street (Trealaw) **14** E2
Charles Street (Treherbert) ..**7** D6
Charles Street (Tylorstown) **12** E1
Charlotte Gardens **20** F3
Charnwood Court...............**38** F1
Chartist Road **35** C4
Chase View **19** C5
Chatham **43** C5
Chatham Place **43** D5
Chatham Street **43** D5
Chepstow Close................**18** F6
Chepstow Court **41** B3
Chepstow Road **8** F3
Cheriton Grove **39** A6
Cherry Court **2** G6/**3** A2
Cherry Drive **2** G6/**3** A3
Cherry Grove **19** C4
Cherry Tree Close (Bedwas)
....**42** F1
Cherry Tree Close (M. Tydfil)
....**18** H2
Cherry Tree Lane **27** C1
Cherry Tree Walk **35** C5
Cherry Tree Way **27** C1
Chester Close **18** E1
Chester Court **41** A3
Chestnut Close (Aberdare) ..**3** A3
Chestnut Close (Machen) ..**43** C5
Chestnut Street **39** A2
Chestnut Way **19** C3
Chestnuts, The **17** D2
Chevron Street **14** G2
Christopher Terrace...........**21** B2
Church Avenue **2** G3
Church Close..........**33** B2/**34** F6
Church Lane (Nantgarw) ...**18** D1
Church Lane (Nelson) **27** D5
Church Road (Abertridwr)..**40** F5
Church Road (Church Village)
..............................**34** G3/**39** A5

Church Road (Gelligaer) **28** H2
Church Road (M. Tydfil) **18** H3
Church Road (Penderyn).....**1** A5
Church Road (Pentre) **9** A5
Church Road (Tonyrefail) ..**13** C5
Church Row (Aberdare)
.................................**2** H5/**3** A1
Church Row (Dowlais).......**20** F4
Church Street (Bedwas) **42** G1
Church Street (Brynna) **17** A5
Church Street (Cwmparc)**8** E4/F6
Church Street (Dowlais) **19** D5
Church Street (Ferndale)....**10** F4
Church Street (Llantrisant) **35** C3
Church Street (Llwynypia) ..**11** C4
Church Street (Machen) **43** C5
Church Street (Maerdy) **9** A1
Church Street (M. Tydfil) **21** A1
Church Street (Mt. Ash)......**23** D5
Church Street (Pentre) **9** A5
Church Street (Penydarren)
....**19** B5
Church Street (Taff's Well) **38** G6
Church Street (Tonypandy) **11** B6
Church Street (Treherbert) ...**7** C5
Church Street (Treorchy) **8** E4/F6
Church Street (Troedyrhiw) **22** F3
Church Street (Ynysybwl) ..**25** C6
Church Street*, Gelliwastad Rd.
....**32** E2
Church Terrace (Llanharan)
....**17** D5
Church Terrace (M. Tydfil) **21** C5
Church Terrace (Penrhiw-fer)
....**13** C5
Church Terrace (Tylorstown)
....**12** E1
Church Terrace (Ynyshir) ..**12** H6
Church View (Abercanaid) **21** C6
Church View (Brynna) **17** A4
Church View (Tylorstown) ..**12** E2
Church View Close **17** B4
Church Walk **29** A4
Churchfield Estate **20** E1
Churchfield Row **9** A5
Cil Hendy........................**17** C1
Cilfedw...........................**37** A5
Cilfynydd Road **30** G1/H5
Cilhaul **27** B1
Cilhaul Terrace **23** C4
Cilsanws Lane..................**18** G3
Claerwen **28** H3
Claerwen Close **4** F3
Clara Street **8** H5
Clare Road **8** F4
Clare Street **21** B2
Claremont Drive **27** C4
Clarence Street (Aberdare) .**6** E1
Clarence Street (Mt. Ash) ..**23** C4
Clarence Street (Ton Pentre)
....**9** A6
Clark Street **8** F2
Clas Ael y Bryn **25** A4
Clas Gwernifor..................**23** C4
Clas Ty Gelli **30** F3
Clas y Derwen **23** C3
Claude Road **41** D5
Claverton Close................**36** G1
Clayton Crescent **30** E4
Cledwyn Gardens **3** A1
Cledwyn Terrace.........**2** G6/**3** A1
Cliff Street **23** B3
Cliff Terrace **32** F3

Clifton Court......................**3** B3
Clifton Crescent **4** F6
Clifton Road **8** F3
Clifton Row **29** A5
Clifton Street (Aberdare) **3** C3
Clifton Street (Caerphilly) ..**42** E5
Clifton Street (Treorchy) **8** F3
Clifton Terrace **4** F6
Clive Place **2** H5/**3** B1
Clive Street (Aberdare) **2** H5/**3** B1
Clive Street (Caerphilly) **41** D5
Clive Street (Senghenydd)..**40** F2
Clive Terrace **25** C6
Clos Alun **17** A5
Clos Aneurin **39** B2
Clos Brenin **17** A2
Clos Broniestyn **31** D2
Clos Brynmelin **37** A5
Clos Cadwgan **36** F2
Clos Cae Pwll **27** D5
Clos Caer Wern...............**41** C6
Clos Caewal **37** B3
Clos Caradog....................**34** F5
Clos Cefn Glas **36** G2
Clos Collwyn **36** G1
Clos Creyr **34** F4
Clos Cwm Garw...............**41** B4
Clos Cyncoed **41** A2
Clos Darren Las **36** H5
Clos Dwyerw **41** C6
Clos Dyfodwg **36** G1
Clos Enfys **41** B6
Clos Glanyrafon*, Bridge Street
....**24** G1
Clos Guto **42** G4
Clos Gwain Gledyr...........**41** B4
Clos Gwastir **41** B6
Clos Gwent **36** E1
Clos Gwynedd **36** E2
Clos Gwynle **41** B6
Clos Hereford **35** C4
Clos Heulwen **38** G4
Clos Lancaster **35** C4
Clos Leland **35** C4
Clos Llangefni **36** E1
Clos Llewellyn **36** H6
Clos Maedref*, Fisher Hill Way
....**37** C6
Clos Maes Mawr **41** C1
Clos Meiri........................**17** A1
Clos Morgan Gruffydd **40** F5
Clos Myddlyn **36** E1
Clos Nant yr Aber **41** C3
Clos Pandy **42** G1
Clos Pantglas **43** A2
Clos Powys **36** E1
Clos Springfield **35** A5
Clos Tyrywen **42** F1
Clos Waun Ceffyl.............**27** D5
Clos Waun Fach **41** A6
Clos William Price **32** H3
Clos y Carw **33** A2/**36** G1
Clos y Cedr **41** D1
Clos y Coed......................**34** G5
Clos y Dolydd **36** F1
Clos y Gamlas **37** D6
Clos y Gwyddfid...............**37** A4
Clos yr Arad **41** B6
Clos Ysbyty **41** C6
Close, The **3** C4
Cloth Hall Lane **18** H3
Clover Road......................**19** A3
Club Row **9** C6/**11** A2

Club Street **3** D5
Clun Avenue **17** B1
Clun Crescent **17** B1
Clwyd Avenue **4** G3
Clydach Close **30** F4
Clydach Court **13** D1
Clydach Road (Tonypandy)
....**12** G2
Clydach Row (Ynysybwl) ..**25** B5
Clydach Terrace **25** C5
Clyne Cottages **12** H2
Clyngwyn Road **7** A3
Clyngwyn Terrace **7** A3
Cobden Place*, Alma St......**21** B1
Cobden Street **5** D1
Coed Bychan Crescent **17** D4
Coed Cae..........................**42** F4
Coed Dowlais **34** G5/H5
Coed Gethin **41** C1
Coed Isaf Road **31** C3
Coed Leddyn **41** C1
Coed Morgannwg Way **3** B4
Coed Pwll.........................**42** F3
Coed y Broch **34** G5
Coed y Lan Road.............**30** F4
Coed y Llinos...................**41** B4
Coed y Llyn **37** A5
Coed y Pandy **42** G1
Coed y Pica*, Llan Road....**40** G6
Coed y Wennol **41** B5
Coed yr Eos......................**41** B4
Coed yr Esgob...................**35** C3
Coed yr Onnen **41** C6
Coedcae Back...................**20** G3
Coedcae Court*, Court Terrace
....**21** B1
Coedcae Road (Abertridwr)
....**40** G6
Coedcae Road (Trehafod)..**29** B5
Coedcae Row **20** H3
Coedcae Terrace.................**5** C4
Coedcae*, Station Ter. **20** G3
Coedglas **2** E3
Coedmeyrick Close **18** F5
Coedpenmaen Close **32** F2
Coedpenmaen Road
.............................**30** G6/**32** F1
Coffins Row*, Dynevor St....**18** G1
Coggins Close **41** B6
Colbourne Road.................**36** F1
Coldra Road **7** A2
Cole Court **42** F3
Coleridge Gardens **43** C2
College Street **3** D3
College Way*, Cardiff Rd...**32** H6
Collenna Road **16** G3
Colliers Avenue **17** C6
Colliers Cottages **28** F6
Colliers Way **11** B5
Colliery Street **29** C5/**31** A1
Collins Close **7** B5
Collins Terrace **32** G5
Colly Cottages **28** G5
Colly Row **28** G5
Column Street **8** F2
Commerce Place **4** E6
Commercial Place **25** D1
Commercial Road ..**43** B5/D6
Commercial Street (Aberdare)
....**3** C3
Commercial Street (Beddau)
....**33** D5

Commercial Street (Bedlinog)
..................................28 G6
Commercial Street
(Blaenllechau) 10 F3
Commercial Street (Llantrisant)
..................................35 D3
Commercial Street (Mt. Ash)
..................................23 B2
Commercial Street (Nelson)
..................................28 E5
Commercial Street (Senghenydd)
..................................40 E2
Commercial Terrace 27 A3
Common Approach ..33 C6/36 F1
Common Road...................32 F2
Compton Road 13 B1
Concorde Drive 16 H2
Concrete Houses 14 E2
Coniston Rise 4 F4
Consort Street 23 C4
Constantine Court 13 C4
Conway Close 30 E4
Conway Court 41 A3
Conway Crescent 34 H3
Conway Drive 4 G4
Conway Grove 18 F6
Conway Road 8 F3
Conybeare Street 23 B3
Cooperative Cottages (Teorchy)
....................................8 E4
Cooperative Cottages*, East Av.
....................................3 B3
Cooperative Street 8 H6
Coopers Place 41 B6
Coplestone Street 23 B4
Copley Street....................23 C2
Coppice, The (Pontyclun) ...17 D1
Coppice, The (Tonteg).......39 A5
Copse, The 19 A1
Corbett Crescent 42 E6
Corbett Grove 41 B6
Corbett Street 7 D5
Corbetts Lane 41 D1
Corner House Street 2 H3
Cornfield Rise 42 G1
Cornwall Road..................13 C3
Coronation Place 24 F1
Coronation Road 15 A3
Coronation Street (Tonypandy)
..................................13 D4
Coronation Street (Trethomas)
..................................43 A2
Coronation Terrace (Heolgerrig)
..................................18 F1
Coronation Terrace (Pontypridd)
..................................30 G6
Coronation Terrace (Porth) 14 H2
Coronation Terrace
(Senghenydd) 40 E2
Corporation Street...........19 D6
Coryton Crescent 37 D4
Coryton Drive 37 D4
Coryton Interchange 37 D3
Coryton Rise 37 D4
Cottage Home Flats 4 H5
Cottesmore Way 36 E5
Cottrell Street 22 G6
Council Street 19 D4
Country View 39 B3
Court House Street 32 E3
Court Place 11 A6
Court Road 41 C3
Court Street (M. Tydfil) 21 A2

Court Street (Tonypandy)
..........................11 A6/12 H2
Court Terrace 21 B1
Court, The*, Glyntaf Road ..32 H3
Courtland Terrace 21 B1
Courtland Villas*, Windsor Ter.
..................................21 B1
Cowbridge Road (Pontyclun)
..................................17 A3
Cowbridge Road (Talbot Grn.)
..............................35 A5/A6
Crabapple Close 19 B3
Crabtree Road..................13 C2
Crabtree Walk 18 H2
Craig Castell 37 A5
Craig y Darren 2 F6
Craig y Llyn Crescent 4 F3
Crawford Close 36 G1
Crawshay Road 13 C3
Crawshay Street (Hirwaun) ..1 A1
Crawshay Street (Pentre) ...9 A5
Crawshay Street (Ynysybwl)
..................................29 C1
Crescent Road 41 D4
Crescent Street 24 G2
Crescent, The (Aberdare) ...2 F6
Crescent, The (Bedwas) ...42 H1
Crescent, The (Caerphilly) 41 C3
Crescent, The (Machen) ...43 B5
Cressely Villas*, Cardiff Road
..................................23 C3
Cribyn Ddu Street 29 C1
Criccieth Grove 18 E6
Crichton Street (Treherbert) 7 C5
Crichton Street (Treorchy) ..8 F2
Crocketts Place 31 C1
Croescade Lane 33 A1/34 E5
Croescade Road 33 D6
Croft Cottages 15 A6
Cromer Street 6 F2
Cromwell Street 19 B6
Cross Blanche Street 20 G3
Cross Brook Street 7 A2
Cross Francis Street 20 E3
Cross Houlson Street........20 F3
Cross Inn Road 35 D4
Cross Ivor Terrace 20 E2
Cross King Street..............20 F1
Cross Lake Street 10 F4
Cross Margaret Street (3) ..19 B5
Cross Mary Street 21 C1
Cross Morgan Street*,
Morgan Street 19 B5
Cross Morlais Street 20 E3
Cross Mount Pleasant......22 G3
Cross Row 13 C3
Cross Street (Abercynon) ..26 E2
Cross Street (Aberdare) 3 C4
Cross Street (Aberfan) 24 G2
Cross Street (Abertridwr) ..40 F5
Cross Street (Bedwas) 42 H1
Cross Street (Cilfynydd) ...30 H4
Cross Street (Clydach Vale)
..................................12 G2
Cross Street (Dowlais).....20 F3
Cross Street (Ferndale) ...10 F4
Cross Street (Glynfach) ...14 H4
Cross Street (Hirwaun) 1 A2
Cross Street (Mt. Ash) 24 E6
Cross Street (Pontypridd) ..32 F1
Cross Street (Porth) 14 H3
Cross Street (Senghenydd) 40 F2
Cross Street (Tongwynlais) 37 B3

Cross Street (Tonypandy) ..13 C3
Cross Street (Treharris).....27 B2
Cross Street (Ynyshir).......12 H6
Cross Street (Ystrad) 9 C6/11 A2
Cross Thomas Street.........21 B1
Crossbank Street..............32 E2
Crossways Street..............32 F1
Crosswood Street 8 G2
Crown Avenue 8 E1
Crown Hill 33 A2/36 H1
Crown Hill Drive 33 B2/36 H1
Crown Row 4 G5
Crown Terrace 8 E1
Crown Walk 43 D5
Crud yr Awel 7 C5
Crwys Crescent 39 C3
Crystal Wood Drive 17 C1
Cuckoofield Close 37 A4
Cules Terrace*, Riverside Street
..................................38 F4
Curre Street 4 E5
Cwm Alarch 6 H4
Cwm Alarch Close..............6 H4
Cwm Eithin 27 D6
Cwm Fedw 43 C4
Cwm Glo Road 18 F1
Cwm Gwynlais...................37 C3
Cwm Hwnt 1 C5
Cwm Hyfryd 16 E4
Cwm Isaac..........................1 D5
Cwm Nant y Felin 41 B6
Cwm Nant yr Hwch 2 F4
Cwm Nofydd Lane 43 A6
Cwmaman Road 5 D1
Cwmbach New Road 4 G5
Cwmbach Road...................3 D3
Cwmdare Road 2 F6
Cwmddu Road 22 F3
Cwmneol Place 5 B3
Cwmneol Street...................5 C3
Cwmsaerbren Flats 7 C5
Cwmsaerbren Street...........7 C5
Cwmynysminton Road........2 F1
Cwrt Alun Lewis..................5 B3
Cwrt Bryn Cynon 26 E2
Cwrt Bryn Isaf 1 D5
Cwrt Coed y Brenin 34 G5
Cwrt Draw Llyn 41 C6
Cwrt Faenor 36 E2
Cwrt Fforest 23 D3
Cwrt Glanrhyd 1 D5
Cwrt Glanwern 4 G5
Cwrt Glyndwr 32 F5
Cwrt Illytd 36 H2
Cwrt Isaf 36 H2
Cwrt Llandewi 4 E6
Cwrt Llanfabon 41 C2
Cwrt Llanwonno 23 B4
Cwrt Maes Cynon 33 D5
Cwrt Pentwyn 33 D5
Cwrt Tre Aman 6 E1
Cwrt Twyn Rhyd 1 D5
Cwrt Ty Mawr....................42 F5
Cwrt y Garth 36 F2
Cwrt y Goedwig.....33 A1/34 E6
Cwrt y Mynydd 37 A5
Cwrt y Waun 36 F2
Cwrt Ynysmeurig 26 G5
Cwrt yr Efail 34 H5
Cyfarthfa Gardens 18 H4
Cyfarthfa Road 19 A6
Cymmer Road 14 F2
Cymric Close 1 D3

Cyncoed 25 A4
Cynllan Avenue 17 C6
Cynllwyndu Road 11 D1
Cynon Close (Beddau) 36 F1
Cynon Close (Trecynon)
....................................2 H5/3 B1
Cynon Cottages 26 G5
Cynon Street 4 E6
Cynon Terrace (Hirwaun) 1 B2
Cynon Terrace (Mt. Ash) ...24 E6
Cynon View 30 H6
Cypress Close 19 B3
Cypress Court 3 A3
Cypress Street...................39 A2
Cyrch y Gwas Road 32 G4
Cyres Street 19 D5

D

Daffodils, The 18 G1
Dalton Close 21 C2
Dan Caerlan 35 D3
Dan y Banc Cottages........37 B2
Dan y Bryn Avenue 37 A5
Dan y Bryn Close...............37 A5
Dan y Coed (Mt. Ash) 23 C2
Dan y Coed (Ystrad)..9 D6/11 A2
Dan y Coedcae Road 31 D4
Dan y Cribyn 29 C2
Dan y Deri Cottages*,
Hamilton Street 23 B3
Dan y Deri Lane 18 H4
Dan y Felin 35 C3
Dan y Gaer Road 28 H3
Dan y Graig (Abertridwr) ...40 G5
Dan y Graig (Ystrad)..9 D6/11 A2
Dan y Graig Heights 35 B3
Dan y Graig Terrace 10 G4
Dan y Parc........................19 C6
Dan y Parc View 19 D6
Dan y Rhiw 5 B3
Dan y Twyn (Church Village)
....................................34 E3
Dan y Twyn (Treharris) 27 B4
Dan yr Allt Close 39 B2
Dan yr Ardd 41 B6
Dan yr Heol 2 E3
Dane Street 19 B6
Dane Terrace 19 B5
Daniel Street 4 G4
Daniels Row 13 C2
Danybryn (Gilfach Goch) ...15 A3
Danybryn (Pontyclun) 17 A2
Danybryn (Radyr) 37 B6
Danybryn Villas 32 F4
Danycoed 42 E6
Danycoed Terrace ...11 A6/12 H2
Danyderi Street 5 D1
Danyderi Terrace...............22 H6
Danygraig (Gilfach Goch) ..15 B3
Danygraig (Trethomas) 43 C2
Danygraig Cottages..........14 E5
Danygraig Crescent 35 B4
Danygraig Drive 35 B4
Danygraig Road 17 D4
Danygraig Street 31 D4
Danygraig Terrace (Llanharan)
....................................17 D5
Danygraig Terrace (Llantrisant)
....................................36 E4
Danygraig Terrace (Tonypandy)
....................................11 A5
Danygraig Terrace (Trebanog)
....................................14 F5

Danygraig Terrace (Ynyshir) 12 G5
Danylan Road 31 C2
Danyronen 18 F1
Danywern Terrace 9 C5/11 A2
Dare Court 2 F6
Dare Road 2 E6
Dare Villas (Aberdare) 3 B3
Dare Villas (Tylorstown) 12 E1
Darran Park 30 F6
Darran Road 23 B3
Darran Terrace 10 F5
Darren Close 42 G2
Darren Court 30 F4
Darren Ddu Road 30 F6
Darren Las 24 H3
Darren View 19 D6
David Dower Close 26 G5
David Price Street 3 C4
David Street (Aberdare) 2 H6/3 B2
David Street (Blaenrhondda) 7 A2
David Street (Cwmdare) 2 E6
David Street (Cwmparc) 8 F6
David Street (M. Tydfil) 21 B2
David Street (2) (Morganstown) 19 B6
David Street (Penygraig) ...13 C3
David Street (Tonypandy) 11 A6/12 H2
David Street (Treherbert) 7 C5
Davids Court 17 B1
Davies Close 14 E2
Davies Drive 41 D2
Davies Place 14 G1
Davies Row 1 A2
Davies Street (Dowlais) 20 F3
Davies Street (Porth) 14 G2
Davies Street (Tonypandy) 11 A6
Davis Street (Aberdare) 4E5
Dawkins Place 2 F4
De Barri Street 34 H1
De Clare Drive 37 C6
De Winton Field 11 B6
De Winton Street 11 B6
De Winton Terrace 11 A6
Dean Street 3 C3
Deere Road 33 B2
Dehewydd Isaf 33 B1/34 F5
Dehewydd Lane 33 B1/34 F5
Delfryn (Llwydcoed) 4 E4
Delfryn (Pontyclun) 17 D1
Dell, The 34 H2
Delwyn Terrace 7 A6
Denbigh Close 34 H3
Denbigh Court (Caerphilly) 41 A3
Denbigh Court (Hirwaun) 1 D2
Dennithorne Close 20 G4
Depot Road 3 C3
Deri Terrace 12 E3
Derlwyn 1 D3
Derwen Aur 14 H2
Derwen Road (Pontyclun) ..17 B2
Derwen Road (Ystrad) 9 D6
Derwendeg Avenue 30 F4
Derwent Drive 4 G4
Derwydd Road 13 B1
Despenser Avenue 35 C4
Devonshire Drive 1 A1
Dewi Street 30 G6
Diamond Close 41 C3
Diana Street 22 F3
Dickens Court 43 D2

Dillington Terrace 25 A1
Dilwyn Street 23 D6
Dilys Street 7 A6
Dinam Park 8 H6
Dinam Park Avenue 8 H6/9 A6
Dinas Isaf Cottages 13 D5
Dinas Road 13 C1/C3/14 E2
District Street 19 D5
Dixon Street 19 B6
Dock Cottages*, Lock St. ..26 H4
Doddington Place 32 F1
Dol Fran 42 G3
Dol y Felin (Caerphilly) 42 E4
Dol y Felin (Creigiau) 36 H6
Dol y Llan 17 D1
Dol y Pandy 42 F1
Dol y Paun 41 B5
Dol yr Eos 42 F3
Dolcoed 2 H2
Dolgellau Avenue 34 H3
Dolgwilym Street 12 E4
Dolgynog 1 A4
Dolycoed Terrace 10 G6
Donald Street (Abercanaid) 21 C6
Donald Street (Nelson) 27 D5
Dorothy Street (Gelli) 9 B6
Dorothy Street (Pontypridd) 32 F1
Dover Place 3 B3
Dover Street (Gelli) 9 B6
Dover Street (Mt. Ash) 23 B3
Dover Terrace*, High St. 3 C3
Dowlais Street 3 B3
Dranllwyn Close 43 B5
Dranllwyn Lane 43 A4/B5
Drill Hall Houses*, Griffith Street 8 H4
Drive, The 17 D3
Dros Col 15 A6
Drovers Way 37 B6
Druids Close 8 G4
Drum Tower View 41 B5
Drysgol Road 37 A6
Duffryn Bach Terrace 34 H4
Duffryn Close 16 F2
Duffryn Cottages 10 F5
Duffryn Crescent 17 B6
Duffryn Fawr 21 D5D6
Duffryn Fawr Estate 21 D6
Duffryn Road (Aberdare) 4 G6
Duffryn Road (Mt. Ash) 23 B1
Duffryn Road (Pentrebach) 21 D5
Duffryn Street (Aberdare) 5 D1
Duffryn Street (Ferndale) ...10 F5
Duffryn Street (Mt. Ash) 23 B3
Duffryn Terrace (Church Village) 34 H5
Duffryn Terrace (Tonyrefail) 16 F2
Duke Street (Aberdare) 3 D3
Duke Street (Treforest) 32 F4
Dumfries Street (Aberdare) ..3 C4
Dumfries Street (Treherbert) 7 C5
Dumfries Street (Treorchy) ..8 F2
Dunraven Court (Caerphilly) 41 A3
Dunraven Court (Tonypandy) 11 A6
Dunraven Court*, Glancynon Ter. 26 G4
Dunraven Crescent 35 A5
Dunraven Place 15 A2
Dunraven Street (Tonypandy) 13 B1

Dunraven Street (Treherbert) 7 B5
Dunraven Terrace 8 F1
Durham Close 18 E1
Dyfed Drive 41 D2
Dyffryn Avenue 39 A1
Dyffryn Crescent 39 A1
Dyffryn Gardens 39 A1
Dyffryn Road 32 H6/39 A2
Dyfodwg Street 8 F3
Dyke Street 21 B2
Dylan Avenue 36 F2
Dylan Drive 41 D3
Dyllas Court 14 H4
Dyllas Road 14 H4
Dynea Close 39 B2
Dynea Road 39 B2
Dynevor Grove 18 F6
Dynevor Street 18 G1/19 B6
Dynevor Terrace 27 D6

E

East Avenue (Aberdare) 3 B3
East Avenue (Bedwas) 42 G1
East Avenue (Caerphilly) ...41 C3
East Court*, East Road 12 E1
East Road 10 G6/12 E2
East Street (Dowlais) 20 F4
East Street (Pontypridd) 32 F1
East Street (Tonypandy) 12 H2
East Street (Tylorstown) 12 E1
East View 42 E5
Eastbourne Place*, Plymouth St. 21 B3
Eastfield Court 35 D5
Eastfield Place 21 B3
Eastfield Terrace 21 B3
Ebenezer Close 27 C2
Ebenezer Road 13 B1
Ebenezer Street (Aberdare) 2 H6/3 B1
Ebenezer Street (Rhydyfelin) 32 H5
Edgar Street 20 E4
Edmondstown Road 14 E5
Edmund Street (Porth) 29 A5
Edmunds Street (Tylorstown) 12 E1
Edward Close 21 C1
Edward Stephens Terrace ..22 H4
Edward Street (Abercynon) 26 G5
Edward Street (Aberdare) 2 H5/3 A1
Edward Street (Maerdy) 9 A1
Edward Street (M. Tydfil) ...20 F1
Edward Street (Mt. Ash) 23 C5
Edward Street (Porth) 14 H3
Edward Street (Treharris) ..27 B3
Edward Terrace (Abertridwr) 40 F4
Edwardian Way 17 D1
Edwards Street (Tonypandy) 11 B5
Edwards Terrace (Bedlinog) 28 G5
Edwards Terrace (Treharris) 27 B4
Edwards Terrace (Trelewis) 27 C1
Edwardsville 26 H1
Efail Shingrig 27 D4
Eglwys Avenue 39 A2
Eglwysilan Road 39 D1/40 E5

Eglwysilan Way 40 F5
Egypt Street (Tonypandy) ..13 D1
Egypt Street (Treforest) 32 G3
Eighth Avenue 19 D3
Eileen Place 7 A4
Eileen Terrace 7 B4
Eirw Road 29 A5
Eisteddfa Road 11 B3
Elan Close 4 G3
Elan Villas 23 C2
Eleanor Street (Tonypandy) 13 B1
Eleanor Street (Treherbert) ..7 D6
Eleventh Avenue 19 D3
Elim Street 19 D4
Elizabeth Close 8 H5
Elizabeth Street (Abercynon) 26 F5
Elizabeth Street (Aberdare) ..3 C4
Elizabeth Street (Pentre) 8 H4
Elizabeth Street (Tonyrefail) 16 F6
Elm Grove (Aberdare) 3 C3
Elm Grove (Caerphilly) 42 F2
Elm Grove (Hirwaun) 1 B1
Elm Grove (M. Tydfil) 19 B4
Elm Grove (Trethomas) 43 A2
Elm Road (Llanharry) 15 A6
Elm Street (Abercwmboi) 6 F2
Elm Street (Ferndale) 10 F4
Elm Street (Gilfach Goch) ..15 A5
Elm Street (Rhydyfelin) 39 A2
Elm Street (Troedyrhiw) 22 G3
Elm Wood Drive 15 D5
Elmgrove Close 30 E4
Elms Park 17 D2
Elwyn Drive 21 B1
Ely Street 13 A1
Ely Terrace 13 C3
Ely Valley Road 16 G6/35 B4
Emanuel Close 41 B6
Emlyn Close 16 F5
Emlyn Drive 41 D3
Emlyn Terrace (Clydach Vale) 12 F2
Emlyn Terrace (4) (M. Tydfil) 19 B5
Emmanuel Close 7 C5
Energlyn Close 41 C3
Energlyn Court 41 C3
Energlyn Crescent 41 C3
Energlyn Terrace 41 C3
Enid Street 13 D1
Enoch Morrell Close 22 G2
Ernest Street 21 B2
Erw Fach 34 F4
Erw Hir 35 D4
Erw Las (M. Tydfil) 18 H6
Erw Las (Penywaun) 2 E3
Ethan Arcade 21 A1
Etna Terrace 15 B3
Eva Street 23 B3
Evan Street 27 B2
Evans Square 30 G6
Evans Terrace (Abercynon) 26 G5
Evans Terrace (Blaen Clydach) 12 G2
Evans Terrace (M. Tydfil) ..21 B2
Evans Terrace (Trealaw) ...13 D1
Evergreen Court 16 H2
Ewenni Fach 17 D5
Excelsior Terrace 9 C3

Exeter Close.....

Exeter Close 18 E2
Exhibition Row....................2 H3

F

Factory Lane 31 D3
Fair View (Gilfach Goch) 15 B1
Fair View (Porth) 14 H3
Fair View Close 17 B2
Fair View Estate 18 F5
Fair View Terrace (Treharris)
............................27 A4
Fairfield Close (Cwmbach) ..4 F4
Fairfield Close (Rhydyfelin) 39 A3
Fairfield House 13 D1
Fairfield Lane...................39 A3
Fairhill Drive 39 A6
Fairland Close 36 E4
Fairmound Place 39 A6
Fairoak Close 3 A3
Fairoak Cottages 36 F2
Fairview (Beddau) 33 D6
Fairview (Hirwaun) 1 A1
Fairview (Penrhiw-fer) 13 D5
Fairview Houses 18 G3
Fairview Terrace (Abercynon)
............................26 H4
Fairview Terrace (M. Tydfil) 21 B2
Fairway Drive 41 C1
Fairways View 35 A4
Fanheulog 35 B5
Fardre Court 34 G3
Fardre Crescent 34 H4
Farm Close 40 G5
Farm Road (Aberdare) 6 E1
Farm Road (Caerphilly) 42 F5
Farm Road (Gelli) 9 A6
Farm Road (Heolgerrig)...18 F1
Farm Terrace 18 F1
Fell Street 27 B2
Fenwick Street.................12 E4
Fern Bank 24 H2
Fern Crescent 3 A3
Fern Hill 9 B6
Fern Street 15 B5
Fern Terrace 12 H2
Ferndale Court...............10 F4
Ferndale Hotel Flats*, Duffryn St.
............................10 F5
Ferndale House 10 F4
Ferndale Road................12 E3
Fernhill............................6 H3
Fernhill Close 22 G3
Fernhill Terrace 26 H1
Fernleigh Place 1 C3
Ferns, The 27 C3
Ffaldau Terrace 9 D3
Ffaldcaiach Cottages......27 D3
Fforch Close 8 F1
Fforchaman Road 5 C3
Fforchaman Street............5 B3
Fforchneol Row 5 C2
Ffordd Catraeth 30 H6
Ffordd Cefn yr Hendy 17 D1
Ffordd Dinefwr 36 H6
Ffordd Erw*, Heol Ysgubor 41 C6
Ffordd Eynon Evans 41 A1
Ffordd Gerdinan 39 A5
Ffordd Glas y Dorlan.........36 G2
Ffordd Gower Davies 29 C2
Ffordd Gwynno 36 G2
Ffordd Las (Abertridwr) 40 G5
Ffordd Las (Radyr) 37 A6
Ffordd Llanbad 15 C5

Ffordd Morganwg 37 D6
Ffordd Penrhos 41 B5
Ffordd Taliesin................30 H5
Ffordd Talygarn 17 B2
Ffordd Tirwaun..................4 F5
Ffordd Traws Cwm 41 B6
Ffordd Tryweryn 30 H6
Ffordd y Bedol 30 F3
Ffordd y Berllan 37 A4
Ffordd y Capel 34 F2
Ffordd y Dderwen 6 H1
Ffordd y Gollen 34 H2
Ffordd y Treforgan...........37 A3
Ffordd yr Afon 38 G6
Ffordd yr Ywen 39 A5
Fforest Cottages 37 C1
Fforest Road (Llanharry) ...15 B6
Fforest Road (Mt. Ash) 23 C3
Ffos Close 27 D5
Ffos y Cerridden 27 D6
Ffrwd Amos Cottages 13 C2
Ffrwd Crescent 23 B2
Ffrwd Road 18 F3
Ffrwd Terrace 1 B2
Ffwrd Street 6 E1
Ffwrwm Road 43 B5
Ffynnon Bwla Road..........39 D2
Ffynnon Las 11 B2
Ffynnon Tudful................19 B6
Ffynon Ffigys Cottages*,
Main Road 38 E4
Fiddlers Elbow 27 A5
Field Street (Tonypandy) ...13 C3
Field Street (Trelewis) 27 C2
Fife Street 26 G4
Fifth Avevue 19 C3
Finchley Close 22 F3
Fir Grove Street................8 H3
Fir Street 10 F3
Fir Tree Close 19 B3
Fir Tree Drive 27 A3
Fir Tree View 19 C5
Firbanks Way..................35 A4
First Avenue (Caerphilly) ...41 C3
First Avenue (M. Tydfil) 19 C3
Fisher Hill Way 37 C6
Fitzwilliam Close 36 E5
Fleming Walk 34 F4
Florence Grove 41 D5
Foel View Close 33 A1/34 E5
Ford Road (Pontypridd)....31 D2
Ford Road (Upper Boat) ...39 C5
Fords Row 14 F3
Forest Farm Road 37 C5
Forest Grove (Mt. Ash) 26 H2
Forest Grove (Treforest) ...32 G5
Forest Hills Drive 35 A5
Forest Road (Beddau) 36 F1
Forest Road (Treforest)....32 G4
Forest Road (Treharris).....27 B1
Forest View (Glyncoch) 30 E4
Forest View (Mt. Ash) 6 G4
Forest View (Talbot Grn.) ..35 C5
Forest Walk 35 A4
Forestry Houses 17 A1
Forge Place 3 D2
Forge Road 43 C5
Forge Row 6 E1
Forge Street......................9 A4
Forge Trip 3 D2
Forge View 5 D1
Forman Place 19 C6
Forrest Houses 12 G2

Forsythia Close 19 A3
Fothergill Crescent 19 D6
Fothergill Street (Aberdare)..3 D2
Fothergill Street (M. Tydfil) 19 D6
Fothergill Street (Treforest) 32 G4
Founders Row 2 H4
Foundry Houses 39 B3
Foundry Place (Pontypridd) 32 F1
Foundry Place (Porth) 14 H4
Foundry Road (Hirwaun) 1 A2
Foundry Road (Pontypridd)
............................31 C2
Foundry Road (Tonypandy)
............................13 B1
Foundry Terrace 23 C3
Foundry View 5 D2
Fountain Street (Ferndale)..10 F4
Fountain Street (Mt. Ash) ..23 B3
Fountain Street (Trehafod)
............................29 C5/31 A1
Fourth Avenue 19 C3
Fox Street (Mt. Ash) 23 C2
Fox Street (Treharris) 27 B2
Foxall Cottages 38 E4
Francis Street (Clydach Vale)
............................12 G1
Francis Street (Dowlais) ...20 E3
Francis Street (Ferndale)...10 F4
Francis Street (Rhydyfelin) 39 A3
Francis Street (Tonyrefail) ..16 F5
Francis Terrace (Dowlais) ..20 E1
Francis Terrace (Pontypridd)
............................30 G6
Frederick Street (Aberdare)
............................2 H6/3 B2
Frederick Street (Ferndale) 10 F4
Fron Terrace 32 F1
Fron Villas*, Campbell Ter. 23 B2
Fronheulog Villas*, Aberfan Rd.
............................22 G6
Fronwen Terrace 19 D5
Furnace Road 12 E3
Furnace Row 22 F1
Furnace Terrace 41 B3

G

Gadlys Gardens 3 C3
Gadlys Road 3 B2
Gadlys Street....................3 B3
Gadlys Terrace 3 B3
Gadlys Uchaf 3 B1
Gaer Place 28 H3
Galon Uchaf Road...........19 C4
Gamlyn Terrace.................1 C3
Garden Street 20 F3
Gardens, The..................27 B4
Garfield Flats*, Tyntaldwyn Road
............................22 G2
Garth Avenue 30 E4/F4
Garth Close 37 A3
Garth Cottages 19 D6
Garth Estate 40 E5
Garth Grove 1 A1
Garth Hill 38 E5
Garth Llwyd....................42 G3
Garth Newydd 38 F6
Garth Olwg 38 E4
Garth Road 13 D1
Garth Street (3) (M. Tydfil) 19 B6
Garth Street (Taff's Well) ..38 G6
Garth Terrace (Bedlinog) ..28 G6
Garth Terrace (M. Tydfil) ...19 D6

Garth View (Beddau)........33 C6
Garth View (Bedwas) 42 G1
Garth View (Church Village)
............................34 G5
Garth View (M. Tydfil) 19 D6
Garth View (Nantgarw) 38 G1
Garth View (Taff's Well)....38 F5
Garth Villas (Abertridwr) ...40 F5
Garth Villas (Taff's Well) ...38 F6
Garth Villas*, Pendarren Road
............................19 C6
Garth Wen......................13 D1
Garth, The 40 E5
Garwellt...........................1 D3
Gas Road 32 E2
Gasworks Road 4 F6
Gate Street*, Riverside Pk. 19 B6
Gelli Aur 2 F6
Gelli Crossing 9 B5
Gelli Dawel 41 C3
Gelli Ddu 39 D4
Gelli Deg (Caerphilly) 41 C2
Gelli Deg (Rhydyfelin) 39 B3
Gelli Deg (Tonyrefail) 16 F5
Gelli Estate 15 B6
Gelli Fedi Rise 17 B4
Gelli Fron 9 A6
Gelli Isaf 2 H4
Gelli Road (Gelli) 9 A6
Gelli Road (Llanharry) 15 B6
Gelli Road (Tonypandy).....13 B1
Gelli Road (Ynysybwl) 25 C6
Gelli Seren......................16 E4
Gelli Terrace (Gelli) 9 B6
Gelli Terrace (Senghenydd)
............................40 G4
Gelli'r Felin 41 C3
Gelli'r Haidd 16 F5
Gelliarael Road 15 A4
Gelliargwellt Road 28 H5
Gellidawel Flats 16 H3
Gellidawel Road 32 H5
Gellideg 18 H6
Gellideg Road 31 D3
Gellifaelog Old Road 20 E4
Gellifaelog Terrace*,
Gellifaelog Old Road ..20 E4
Gellifedi Road 17 B4
Gelligaer Road 27 D3/28 F3
Gelligaled Road 9 C5/11 A2
Gelligron Estate 11 A5
Gellihirion Industrial Estate Road
............................39 B3
Gelliseren Close 16 E5
Gelliwasted Grove 32 E2
Gelliwion Road 31 A5
Gelliwion Woods 31 D3
Gelynis Terrace 37 A3
Gelynis Terrace North 37 A3
Gelynog Court 33 C5
Gelynog Villas 33 C5
George Close...................38 F6
George Street (Aberdare) 4 E3
George Street (Bedlinog) ..28 H5
George Street (Blaenllechau)
............................10 F4
George Street (Dowlais) ...20 F4
George Street (Llantrisant) 35 C5
George Street (Tonypandy) 13 C3
George Street (Treherbert) ..7 B6
George Terrace (Mt. Ash) ..23 D5
George Terrace*, Dyffryn Road
............................21 B6

Georges Terrace (Tonypandy) 11 A6/12 H2
Georgetown 38 F6
Georgetown Villas*,
  Nantygwenith Street....19 B6
Georgian Way 17 D1
Ger y Bont 1 D4
Ger yr Afon (Aberdare) 4 E6
Ger yr Afon (Coed y Cwm) 30 F3
Gernant Lane.....................18 E2
Gersanws 18 G3
Gertrude Street 26 G5
Gerybont 1 D3
Gethin Place 21 C6
Gethin Road (Tonypandy)..13 C3
Gethin Road (Treorchy) 8 G2
Gethin Street 21 C6
Gethin Terrace...................29 A4
Giles Court..........................3 B2
Gilfach Cynon 21 B2
Gilfach Maen Isaf Cottages 27 C1
Gilfach Road (Tonypandy)..13 A1
Gilfach Road (Tonyrefail)...16 E3
Gillar Street 21 A1
Gilmour Street 11 B6
Glade, The...........................3 D3
Gladstone Street (Aberdare) 4 F6
Gladstone Terrace (M. Tydfil)
  ....21 B3
Gladstone Street (Mt. Ash) 23 C5
Gladstone Terrace (Mt. Ash)
  ....23 C5
Glamorgan Court (Aberaman)
  ....4 E6
Glamorgan Court (Treforest)
  ....32 F5
Glamorgan Street (Aberdare)
  ....4 E6
Glamorgan Street (Mt. Ash)
  ....23 D6
Glamorgan Terrace
  (Gilfach Goch) 15 B3
Glamorgan Terrace
  (Llwynypia)..................11 A5
Glamorgan Terrace
  (Williamstown) 13 D5
Glan Creigiau 36 G6
Glan Felin 39 A3
Glan Ffrwd (Caerphilly) 41 B1
Glan Ffrwd (Porth)...........14 F5
Glan Mafon 27 A5
Glan Nant Close 41 D6
Glan Road 3 A3
Glan y Ffordd....................38 F4
Glan y Llyn 12 G2
Glan y Nant 39 B2
Glan yr Afon (Aberfan) 24 G3
Glan yr Afon (Gwaelod-y-garth)
  ....38 E5
Glan yr Afon (Machen) 43 C5
Glan yr Afon (Pontyclun)...17 B2
Glan yr Afon*, Dynevor St. 18 G1
Glan yr Ely 35 A1
Glanaman Road 5 A3
Glanant Street 1 B3
Glancynon Street..............23 C5
Glancynon Terrace (Abercynon)
  ....26 G4
Glancynon Terrace (Aberdare)
  ....4 E6
Glandwr Terrace 11 A5
Glanffrwd Terrace 25 B5
Glanlay Street 24 E6

Glanmorlais 20 F1
Glannant Road 15 A3
Glannant Street (Aberdare)..3 C4
Glannant Street (Tonypandy)
  ....13 C2
Glanrhyd Street 5 A3
Glanselsig Terrace 7 A6
Glantaff Road....................22 F3
Glanville Terrace 9 C3
Glanynys Cottages 3 D3
Glanynys House 3 D3
Glanyrafon 8 E2
Glas Cwm 30 F3
Glasbrook Terrace 24 E6
Glasfryn.............................2 G6
Glasfryn Terrace 12 E2
Glasier Road 21 B2
Glaslyn Drive 4 F3
Glebe Road 43 A2
Glebe Street 42 H1
Glebeland Cottages...........38 E2
Glebeland Place 21 A1
Glebeland Street 21 A1
Glen Close 23 A2
Glen View Place 10 E3
Glen View Street 11 A6
Glen View Villas................27 B3
Glenavon Terrace 15 B3
Glenboi 6 H3
Glenbrook 23 A2
Glendower Street..............20 E3
Glenrhondda Court 7 C5
Glenview 12 F4
Gloucester Street 3 C3
Gloucester Terrace 26 E2
Glymil Close 19 D6
Glyn Bargoed Road...........27 C3
Glyn Drew 41 D3
Glyn Rhyd 41 C4
Glyn Street (Porth) ..14 H4/29 A5
Glyn Street (Ynysybwl) 29 C1
Glyn Terrace 12 H2
Glyn View (Blaenllechau) ..10 E3
Glyn View (Tonyrefail) 16 H2
Glynbargoed Close 27 C2
Glyncoed 9 B2
Glyncoed Terrace 21 B2
Glyncoli Close 8 G2
Glyncoli Road 8 F2
Glyncornel Close 11 B4
Glynderus Close 21 B4
Glyndwr 9 C6
Glyndwr Avenue 32 H5
Glyndwr Street 24 G1
Glynfach Road..................14 H4
Glyngoch Terrace 30 G4
Glyngwyn Street 23 C4
Glynhafod Street 5 A3
Glynmil Caravan Site........21 C4
Glynmynach Street 29 C1
Glynn Terrace 19 C6
Glynrhondda Street 8 F2
Glyntaff Court 22 G3
Glyntaff Road 32 H3
Gnoll, The 2 H3
Goat Mill Road..................20 E6
Gobaith Terrace 2 F6
Godre'r Coed Road 18 H4
Godreaman Street...............5 D1
Goedig Villas 14 G1
Goitre Coed Isaf 26 H4
Goitre Coed Road 26 H3/27 A4
Goitre Lane 19 B2/C4

Golf Road 4 E2
Golwg y Coed 41 A3
Golwg yr Eglwys 42 G1
Golygfar Eglwys 31 D2
Goodrich Avenue...............42 F5
Goodrich Street 42 E5
Gordon Street (Cwmaman)..5 C2
Gordon Street (Pentre) 8 H5
Gordon Villas 3 D3
Gorsedd Street 23 B3
Gorsedd Terrace 19 C6
Gospel Court 33 C6
Gospel Hall Terrace 3 C2
Gower Davis Court 29 C2
Gower Road.........................4 F3
Grafton Drive 36 E5
Graham Court 42 F4
Graham Street 21 A1
Graham Way 21 A1
Graig Avenue (Abercwmboi) 6 F2
Graig Avenue (Pontypridd) 31 D4
Graig Close 21 B6
Graig Cottages (Caerphilly) 41 A6
Graig Cottages (Miskin).....17 D2
Graig Crescent (Abercwmboi)
  ....6 F2
Graig Crescent (Porth).......14 F5
Graig Ddu 9 B3
Graig Ddu Cottages...........14 E2
Graig Ddu Court 14 E2
Graig Ddu Place 14 E2
Graig Ddu Road 13 D2
Graig Fach 32 H3
Graig Hir 37 A4
Graig Isaf 3 C4
Graig Llwyd 37 A4
Graig Place 3 C4
Graig Road (Abercanaid)...21 B6
Graig Road (Ynyshir)........12 H6
Graig Street (Aberdare) 3 C4
Graig Street (Mt. Ash) 23 B3
Graig Street (Pontygwaith) 11 D3
Graig Street (Pontypridd)...32 E3
Graig Terrace (Abercwmboi) 6 F2
Graig Terrace (Bedlinog)...28 G5
Graig Terrace (Dowlais) 20 E3
Graig Terrace (Ferndale)....10 F5
Graig Terrace (Pontypridd) 32 E3
Graig Terrace (Senghenydd)
  ....40 E1
Graig View (Machen).........43 D5
Graig View (Nantgarw).......38 G1
Graig Wen (Maerdy) 9 B3
Graig y Ddelw............7 A3/B6
Graig y Fedw 40 H6
Graig y Hendre 28 H5
Graig y Mynydd 16 E4
Graig yr Eos Terrace 13 C3
Graig yr Helfa Cottages.....32 G3
Graig yr Helfa Road 32 G3
Graig yr Hesg Place..........30 F6
Graig yr Wylan 41 B5
Graiglwyd............................2 F5
Graigside 38 G3
Graigwen (Morganstown) ..37 A4
Graigwen Cottages 32 G3
Graigwen Crescent 40 G5
Graigwen Parc..................31 D1
Graigwen Place 32 E2
Graigwen Road (Pontypridd)
  ....31 D1
Graigwen Road (Porth) 14 G4
Grand View 13 C4

Grand View Terrace 13 C3
Grange Bungalows (Aberdare)
  ....4 E5
Grange Bungalows (Caerphilly)
  ....41 C4
Grange Close 41 C4
Grange Terrace 11 B5
Grange, The (Caerphilly)...41 C4
Grange, The (Llan. Fardre) 33 A2
Grants Close 37 C3
Granville Terrace...............23 C2
Grasmere Drive...................4 G4
Grawen Houses 18 G3
Grawen Lane.....................18 G3
Grawen Street...................14 G2
Grawen Terrace.................19 B5
Grays Gardens 43 D2
Grays Place 24 H2
Great Street 29 C5/31 A1
Great Western Terrace 35 A5
Green Bank Villas*,
  Woodland Street 23 B2
Green Hill (Ferndale).........10 F4
Green Hill (Pentre).............9 B5
Green Meadow 43 D3
Green Park.....................35 B4/B5
Green Row 43 B5
Green Street 3 C3
Green Villas........................2 H4
Green Wood Drive (Llan. Fardre)
  ....33 A1/34 E6
Green, The (M. Tydfil) 18 H2
Green, The (Radyr) 37 B6
Greenacre Drive (Bedwas) 42 G1
Greenacre Drive (Tonypandy)
  ....13 A1
Greenacre Gardens...........43 A2
Greenacres 36 H6
Greendale Place 37 C3
Greenfield Avenue 30 E4
Greenfield Gardens 21 C5
Greenfield Place 40 E5
Greenfield Street 13 C3
Greenfield Terrace (Abercynon)
  ....26 G4
Greenfield Terrace (Cwmbach)
  ....4 G6
Greenfield Terrace (Cwmparc)
  ....8 E6
Greenfield Terrace (Dowlais)
  ....20 E4
Greenfield Terrace (Mt. Ash)
  ....6 H1
Greenfield Terrace (Pentrebach)
  ....21 D6
Greenfield Terrace*, Merthyr Rd.
  ....22 G2
Greenhill 27 C6
Greenhill Cottages*, Bridge Rd.
  ....4 G5
Greenhill Drive....................4 E6
Greenhill Place 28 H3
Greenlands Road 35 D4
Greenmeadow Close 30 F4
Greenmeadow Cottages 43 D3
Greenmeadow Court 35 D4
Greenmeadow Drive 37 C3
Greenmeadow Terrace 13 C5
Greenway (Caerphilly).......42 E1
Greenway Court 42 G1
Greenways (Aberdare) 4 E2
Greenwood Court 42 F4
Greenwood Drive (Hirwaun) 1 C2

Gresham Place 27 A3
Greyhound Lane*, Heol y Beiliau
.................................35 C4
Greys Place.......................2 H2
Griffin Park 8 H4
Griffith Drive 37 D6
Griffith Street (Aberdare) ...3 C4
Griffith Street (Maerdy) 9 A1
Griffith Street (Pentre) 8 H4
Griffith Terrace (Aberfan) ..24 G1
Griffiths Terrace*, Duffryn Road
.................................21 D6
Groeswen Drive................41 A4
Groeswen Road................41 A4
Grongaer Terrace 32 E3
Grove Estate 43 A1
Grove House Court 12 E4
Grove Park 19 C5
Grove Terrace (Abercwmboi)
...................................6 F2
Grove Terrace (Bedlinog) ..28 G5
Grove Terrace (Llanharan) 17 C4
Grove Terrace (Senghenydd)
.................................40 E2
Grove Terrace (Ynysybwl)..29 C1
Grove, The (Aberdare) 3 C4
Grove, The (Glyncoch) 30 G3
Grove, The (M. Tydfil) 19 C5
Grove, The (Troedyrhiw)....22 G6
Grovefield Terrace.............13 C2
Grover Street....................32 E3
Grovers Close 30 F4
Grovers Field 26 F6/30 F1
Grovers Road*, Abercynon Rd.
.................................30 G3
Gruffydd Drive 41 D2
Guest Cottages 20 F3
Gurney Cottages*, Dover Street
.................................23 B3
Gurnos Farm Cottages 19 A2
Gurnos Road 19 A4
Gwaelod y Foel 34 F5
Gwaelod y Garth Road 39 C5
Gwaelodygarth Close 19 C5
Gwaelodygarth Lane*,
    Gwaelodygarth Rd. 19 C5
Gwaelodygarth Road ...19 B5/C5
Gwaelodygarth Villas*,
    Gwaelodygarth Rd. ...19 C5
Gwalia Grove...................32 H5
Gwalia Place 19 C6
Gwalia Terrace 4 E5
Gwasted 41 D1
Gwaun Bedw 14 H4
Gwaun Hyfryd 42 G3
Gwaun Llwyfen 27 D6
Gwaun Newydd 42 G4
Gwaun Road 32 H5
Gwaun Ruperra Close 35 D3
Gwaun Ruperra Road 35 D3
Gwaun y Cwrt 41 A6
Gwaun y Groes 36 E4
Gwaunfarren Close 19 C4
Gwaunfarren Grove 19 C5
Gwaunfarren Road 19 C5
Gwaunmiskin Road ..33 C6/36 F1
Gwaunrhydd 36 F1
Gwawr Street......................3 D5
Gwendoline Street (M. Tydfil)
.................................19 C5
Gwendoline Street (Treherbert)
...................................7 B4
Gwendoline Terrace 26 G5

Gwenfron Terrace 13 D4
Gwenllian Terrace 34 H1
Gwent Road 39 D6
Gwent Terrace 14 G2
Gwern Avenue..................40 E2
Gwern y Milwr*, Gwern Av. 40 E2
Gwernifor Street 23 B4
Gwernllwyn Close 20 E4
Gwernllwyn Terrace 10 G6
Gwernllwyn Uchaf*, Muriel Ter.
.................................20 F3
Gwernllyn Road 20 F3
Gwili Road 39 C4
Gwilym Street 32 H6/34 H1
Gwilym Terrace 21 B3
Gwlad Du Gwyrdd 15 B5
Gwladys Street (Aberdare) ..2 E4
Gwladys Street (Dowlais) ..19 D4
Gwladys Street (M. Tydfil) ..20 F1
Gwladys Street (Penywaun) 2 E4
Gwyn Drive 41 D3
Gwyn Street 32 G6
Gwynfan Place*, Plymouth St.
.................................21 B3
Gwynfi Terrace 17 D5
Gwynfryn Terrace 33 B1
Gwynne Close 19 D6
Gwynnes Close*, Walter Street
.................................20 E4
Gyfeillon Road 31 B1
Gynor Avenue 14 G1
Gynor Place 12 G6
Gypsy Lane 41 A6

H

Hadrians Close 28 H2
Hafan Heulog 30 F2
Hafan Werdd 42 G3
Hafen Deg 2 H4
Hafod Estate 20 F2
Hafod Lane 29 C4
Hafod Road 29 B5
Hafod Street 21 D6
Hafod Wen (Aberdare).........2 F6
Hafod Wen (Tonyrefail) 16 H2
Hafod, The 20 F2
Haines Close 41 B6
Haldane Court 42 G4
Halifax Terrace 7 A3
Hall Street 3 C3
Halswell Street 25 D1
Haman Place 28 H3
Hamilton Street (Mt. Ash) ..23 B3
Hamilton Street (Pentrebach)
.................................21 D6
Hampton Street 21 B2
Hampton Place 21 B2
Hanbury Close 37 D6
Hankey Place 21 B3
Hankey Terrace 21 B3
Hannah Street 14 H3
Hanover Street 19 B6
Harcombe Road 11 C4
Harcourt Road 23 B2
Harcourt Terrace 23 D5
Harford Close 37 D6
Harlech Court 41 A3
Harlech Drive 18 E6
Harlech House...................37 B5
Harlech Place 3 B4
Harold Street 17 C6
Harriet Street.............2 H5/3 B1
Harriet Town 22 F3

Harris Street 1 A2
Harris View 23 D6
Harrison Street 19 D4
Hartshorn Court.................42 G4
Harvard Road 40 F5
Haul Fron.........................13 C5
Haulfryn 2 E3
Haulwen 2 F6
Haven Close 22 G3
Haven, The 1 A2
Hawarden Place 22 F3
Hawthorn Avenue 19 C4
Hawthorn Cottages*, Fernhill Cl.
.................................22 G3
Hawthorn Crescent 39 B3
Hawthorn Hill 18 H1
Hawthorn Park 17 B5
Hawthorn Rise 2 F6
Hawthorn Road (Llanharry) 15 B6
Hawthorn Road (Nelson)....28 E6
Hawthorn Road (Rhydyfelin)
.................................39 B3
Hawthorn Villas 39 B3
Hawthorne Terrace (Aberdare)
...................................3 D4
Hawthorne Terrace (Mt. Ash)
.................................23 D6
Hawthorns, The 20 E1
Haydn Terrace..................19 D4
Hazel Court 16 H2
Hazel Drive 3 A3
Hazel Grove (Caerphilly) ...42 F2
Hazel Grove (Hendreforgan)
.................................15 C5
Hazel Grove (Trethomas) ..43 A1
Hazel Terrace (Mt. Ash) 23 D6
Hazel Terrace (Troedyrhiw)
.................................22 G2
Hazeldene 15 A6
Heads of the Valleys Road
..........1 C2/18 E5/19 A2/20 G3
Heath Close 4 F4
Heath Crescent*, Graigwen Rd.
.................................31 D2
Heath Terrace (Ynyshir) 12 H5
Heath Terrace*, Graigwen Road
.................................31 D2
Heather Close 13 B1
Heather Road 19 A3
Heather View Road 32 G1
Heather Way 29 A4
Heathfield Crescent 17 B6
Heathfield Road 32 G1
Heathfield Villas 32 G4
Heathlands, The 15 B4/B5
Hebron Villas 26 E2
Heddwch Close 20 E2
Hendre 41 C1
Hendre Gwilym 13 B2
Hendre Road 40 E5
Hendre Terrace 13 C3
Hendrecafn Road 13 B2
Hendredenny Drive 41 A3
Hendrefadog Street 12 E1
Hendreforgan Crescent 15 B5
Hendreselsig 7 A3
Hendrewen Road.................7 A6
Henfron 41 B2
Henllys 14 F6
Henry Richard Street.........22 G3
Henry Street (Aberdare) 4 E5
Henry Street (Mt. Ash).......23 C3
Henry Street (Pontypridd) ..31 C1

Hensol Road (Pontyclun) ..17 C3
Henwysg Close 31 C1
Heol Adam 28 G1
Heol Alfred 9 B2
Heol Aneurin (Caerphilly)
.................................41 B1/B2
Heol Aneurin (Tonyrefail) ..16 G3
Heol ap Pryce 36 F1
Heol Barri 41 C2
Heol Beddau 33 C5
Heol Bedw 14 H5
Heol Berllan 42 E2
Heol Berry 38 F6
Heol Billingsley 38 E1
Heol Bonymaen 20 E1
Heol Bro Wen 42 E3
Heol Brofiscin...................36 F6
Heol Brychan 18 G5
Heol Bryn Fab 18 G5
Heol Bryn Glas 33 B1/34 F5
Heol Bryn Gwyn 1 D3
Heol Bryn Hebog..............18 G5
Heol Bryn Heulog ..33 B1/34 F5
Heol Bryn Man 18 G5
Heol Bryn Padell 18 G5
Heol Bryn Selu 18 G5
Heol Bryn y Gwyddyl........18 G5
Heol Brynhyfryd................33 D5
Heol Brynmor John 34 G4
Heol Brynteg 16 F4
Heol Cae Bach 42 E2
Heol Cae Barrau 41 A6
Heol Cae Celynnen 42 E2
Heol Cae Fan Heulog 42 E2
Heol Cae Maen 42 E2
Heol Caerlan 36 E1
Heol Capel 16 G2
Heol Caradoc 2 E4/F3
Heol Cattwg.....................28 H3
Heol Cawrdaf 36 F1
Heol Cefn yr Hendy 17 C1
Heol Ceiriog 12 F4
Heol Celyn 34 H4
Heol Celynen 29 F3
Heol Clwyddau 36 F1
Heol Clyd 41 A2
Heol Coflorna 27 C3
Heol Coroniad 33 C5
Heol Creigiau 36 H5
Heol Crochendy................24 E2
Heol Cronfa 30 H5
Heol Cwarrel Clark 41 B1
Heol Cwm Ifor 41 A1
Heol Cynllan 17 D6
Heol Dafydd 17 B2
Heol Dderwen 39 A5
Heol Ddeusant 36 F1
Heol Ddu 33 A4
Heol Deg 34 H3
Heol Deri 16 E4
Heol Dewi 17 A5
Heol Dowlais 34 E2
Heol Dyfed (Aberdare).........2 F4
Heol Dyfed (Beddau) 36 E2
Heol Dyfed (Penrhys) 11 C2
Heol Dyfodwg 35 C3
Heol Dyhewydd 33 D6
Heol Edward Lewis 28 H3
Heol Edwards 38 G1
Heol Erw y Rhos 42 E2
Heol Esgyn 1 D5
Heol Fach (Caerphilly).......41 C3
Heol Fach (Nantgarw)........38 G1

Heol Faenor................36 E2
Heol Fawr (Caerphilly)........41 B1
Heol Fawr (Nelson) 28 E6
Heol Fer........................41 B1
Heol Ffrwd Philip 34 F2
Heol Ganol 41 D4
Heol Gelynen................1 D3
Heol Gelynog 36 F1
Heol Gerrig 18 E2
Heol Glan Elai 17 B2
Heol Glannant 13 D5
Heol Gledyr 41 D5
Heol Glyn....................41 C2
Heol Glyncoch 15 C5
Heol Goch*, Main Road......37 A1
Heol Goronwy 12 F4
Heol Graigwen 41 B2
Heol Groeswen 39 D4
Heol Gwaun Rhos 42 E2
Heol Gwrangfryn 1 D6
Heol Gwrgan 33 C6
Heol Gwynno 35 C3
Heol Harry Lewis...........27 D6
Heol Haulfryn 16 F4
Heol Hendy 17 C1
Heol Hensol 36 F1
Heol Heulog 15 A3
Heol Horeb 14 G4
Heol Ida......................33 C6
Heol Illtyd....................35 C3
Heol Ioan 11 C2
Heol Isaf (Llan. Fardre) 36 G2
Heol Isaf (Nelson) 28 E6
Heol Isaf (Radyr) 37 B4
Heol Isaf (Trelewis) 27 C1
Heol Isaf Hendy 17 C2
Heol Iscoed 34 E2
Heol Islwyn (Nelson) 27 D6
Heol Islwyn (Tonyrefail)....16 G2
Heol Johnson..............35 B5
Heol Keir Hardie 2 E4
Heol Las (Caerphilly) 41 C1
Heol Las (Llantrisant) 35 B2
Heol Lewis....................42 G2
Heol Llechau 12 F4
Heol Llwyn Brain 18 G5
Heol Llwyn Deri 18 G5
Heol Llwyn Drysi 18 G5
Heol Llwyn Gollen 18 G5
Heol Llwyn Onnen 18 G5
Heol Llyswen 27 D5
Heol Lodwig 34 G5
Heol Mabon 27 D6
Heol Maerdy 42 G3
Heol Mair.....................11 C2
Heol Miles 35 B5
Heol Miskin 17 B1
Heol Morien 27 C6
Heol Mwyrdy 36 E1
Heol Mynydd (Church Village)
................................34 H4
Heol Mynydd (Cilfynydd) 30 H5
Heol Nant (Aberdare)..........2 F5
Heol Nant (Church Village) 34 H4
Heol Nant (Cilfynydd) 30 H5
Heol Nant Caiach 27 C3
Heol Nantgau 18 G5
Heol Orchwy 8 F2
Heol Pant Gwyn..........15 B6
Heol Pant y Gored.........36 H5
Heol Parc Glas 18 G5
Heol Parc Maen...........18 H5
Heol Parc y Lan...........18 H5

Heol Pardoe....................38 E1
Heol Pen Nant 4 E2
Heol Pen y Bryn 11 C2
Heol Pen y Foel 30 F3
Heol Pen y Parc (Coed y Cwm)
................................30 F2
Heol Pen y Parc (Llantrisant)
................................35 D4
Heol Penallta 28 H3
Heol Pendarren 1 C6
Heol Pendyrus 11 C2/D2
Heol Penmaen...............35 C4
Heol Penrhiw (M. Tydfil) 18 G5
Heol Penrhiw (Mt. Ash) 23 A1
Heol Pentwyn................16 F4
Heol Pwllypant..............41 C2
Heol Pymmer 16 F4
Heol Rhos 41 B4
Heol Rhos Las..............18 G5
Heol Rhosyn 36 G1
Heol Rhyd y Bedd 20 E2
Heol Rhys 4 G5
Heol Robert 17 B2
Heol S. O. Davies 18 G1
Heol Salem 34 H4
Heol Scwrfa 18 G5
Heol Serth 41 A2
Heol Seward 36 E1
Heol Silyn 2 E4
Heol Sticil y Beddau 35 C4
Heol Syr Lewis...............37 A3
Heol Tai Mawr 18 G5
Heol Tasker 27 C6
Heol Teifionydd 11 C2
Heol Tir Bach................41 B2
Heol Tir Coch................34 F2
Heol Tir Gibbon 41 B2
Heol Tir Gwaidd..............11 D2
Heol Ton 16 F4
Heol Trane 16 E4
Heol Trecastell 41 D5
Heol Treferig 36 F1
Heol Trewilliam 13 D5
Heol Twyn Du 18 G5
Heol Ty Aberaman...........6 E1
Heol Ty Crwn 42 E2
Heol Ty Merchant 42 E2
Heol Tyddyn 41 A6
Heol Tyle Du 8 F2
Heol Tyllwyd 16 G2
Heol Tymaen 39 D4
Heol Uchaf (Nelson) 28 E6
Heol Uchaf (Penywaun)....1 B3
Heol Uchel 1 A2
Heol Undeb 36 F1
Heol Waun 16 E4
Heol Waun Fawr 41 B6
Heol Waun Waelod 41 C6
Heol y Beddau..............41 D5
Heol y Beiliau 35 C4
Heol y Berth..................41 C6
Heol y Bryn (Hendreforgan)
................................15 C5
Heol y Bryn (Pontyclun)....17 C1
Heol y Bryn (Rhigos) 1 D5
Heol y Bryn (Rhydyfelin) 39 B1
Heol y Bryniau 20 E1
Heol y Bwnsy 38 F1/39 D4
Heol y Cae...................18 H4
Heol y Carnau 42 E2
Heol y Castell 20 E1
Heol y Clun 36 E1
Heol y Coed (Beddau) 36 E1

Heol y Coed (Nantgarw) 38 G1
Heol y Coed (Pontyclun) 17 C1
Heol y Cwm.................41 C6
Heol y Dderwen.............38 G1
Heol y Ddol 42 E2
Heol y Ddu 41 B6
Heol y De......................1 D5
Heol y Deri...................31 D1
Heol y Derw 15 A3
Heol y Dreflan 42 E2
Heol y Eos 4 E2
Heol y Fedwen 34 H2
Heol y Felin (Caerphilly) 41 C4
Heol y Felin (Pontyclun) 17 B2
Heol y Fforest 37 C1
Heol y Ffynnon (Efail Isaf) ..34 F2
Heol y Ffynnon (Penrhys) ..11 C2
Heol y Foel....................34 F5
Heol y Fro 34 G3
Heol y Gamlas 39 D6
Heol y Gelli 5 D1
Heol y Gledyr................41 D5
Heol y Glyn (Tonyrefail) 16 G3
Heol y Glyn (Trelewis) 27 C3
Heol y Goedwig.............34 G5
Heol y Gogledd 41 B1
Heol y Gors (Caerphilly) 42 E2
Heol y Gors (Nantgarw) 38 G1
Heol y Graig (Llantrisant) ..35 C4
Heol y Graig (Penrhys) 11 D2
Heol y Graig (Rhigos) 1 D5
Heol y Grug 15 C5
Heol y Gyfraith...............35 B4
Heol y Maes 33 B1/34 F5
Heol y Mynach...............25 A4
Heol y Mynydd (Aberdare)....3 B4
Heol y Mynydd (Hendreforgan)
................................15 C5
Heol y Mynydd (M. Tydfil) ..18 G3
Heol y Mynydd (Ystrad).......9 C5
Heol y Nant (Aberdare) 4 E1
Heol y Nant (Caerphilly) 41 D4
Heol y Nant (Gwaelod-y-garth)
................................38 F6
Heol y Parc (Aberdare) 4 E2
Heol y Parc (Caerphilly) 41 D4
Heol y Parc (Efail Isaf) ..34 F1/H6
Heol y Parc (Evanstown) 15 A3
Heol y Parc (Trehafod) 29 B5
Heol y Pia 41 B4
Heol y Plwyf 25 B5
Heol y Pwll 38 F1
Heol y Sarn 35 C1
Heol y Twyn (Aberdare).......2 F5
Heol y Twyn (Wattstown)....12 F4
Heol y Waun (Gelligaer) 28 H3
Heol y Waun (Penrhys) 11 C2
Heol y Wern (Caerphilly) 42 E2
Heol y Wern (Nelson) 28 E5
Heol y Ynys Ddu 41 B6
Heol yr Haul 36 F6
Heol yr Odyn 38 F1
Heol yr Onen 41 D4
Heol yr Orsaf 17 B1
Heol yr Ynys 37 A2
Heol yr Ynys Court 37 A2
Heol yr Ysbyty 41 C6
Heol yr Ysgol 43 A2
Heol Ysgubor 41 C6
Herbert Drive..............41 D2
Herbert Street (Abercynon) 26 G5
Herbert Street (Aberdare) 3 C4
Herbert Street (Treherbert) ..7 D5

Herbert Street (Treorchy)......8 F2
Heritage Court 19 C5
Hermon Close 20 E4
Hermon Flats*, Llewellyn Street
................................12 E3
Hermon Hill 37 B3
Hermon Street..............8 G3
Herons Way..................41 B6
Herrick Place 43 D1
Heulwen Close 20 E2
Hibiscus Court 36 H1
Hickman Street 21 D6
High Close...................27 D6
High Row 23 B1
High Street (Abercanaid) 21 B6
High Street (Aberdare) 3 C3
High Street (Abertridwr) 40 F4/F5
High Street (Bedlinog) 28 H6
High Street (Cefn Coed) 18 H4
High Street (Clydach Vale) 12 F2
High Street (Dowlais)
................................19 D5/20 E4
High Street (Ferndale) 10 F4
High Street (Gilfach Goch) 15 B3
High Street (Hirwaun) 1 A2
High Street (Llantrisant) 35 C3
High Street (M. Tydfil)
................................19 C6/21 A1
High Street (Mt. Ash)........23 B3
High Street (Nelson) 27 C6
High Street (Pontyclun) 17 A3
High Street (Pontypridd) 32 E3
High Street (Porth).........14 G5/H3
High Street (Senghenydd)..40 E2
High Street (Tonyrefail) 16 G3
High Street (Trelewis) 27 C2
High Street (Treorchy)..........8 G3
High Street (Trethomas) 43 B1
High Street (Ynysybwl)
................................25 C6/29 C1
High Street Arcade*, High St.
................................21 A1
High Trees 19 A1
High View Way 30 F4
High Willows 34 G3
Highdale Close 35 D4
Highfield 9 C3
Highfield Close 39 A6
Highfield Terrace 31 D2
Highland Close 21 B2
Highland Place 3 B4
Highland View 21 B2
Highlands Close 16 G2
Highlands, The 16 G2
Hilda Street 32 G6
Hill Crest......................17 B1/B2
Hill Drive..................33 B1/34 F6
Hill Street (Abercynon)........26 F6
Hill Street (Aberdare).........3 D5
Hill Street (Gilfach Goch)...15 B5
Hill Street (Maerdy)..........9 A1
Hill Street (Tonypandy) 13 B2
Hill Street (Treherbert) 7 B5
Hill Street (Troedyrhiw) 22 F3
Hill Terrace 10 G5
Hill Top 2 H4
Hill View 36 F1
Hillbrook Close 3 D5
Hillcrest 19 D3
Hillcrest Avenue..............4 E6
Hillcrest Drive 14 H4
Hillcrest View 9 B3
Hillside (Aberdare)..........2 F6

Hillside (Caerphilly) **42** E6
Hillside (Mt. Ash) **23** C5
Hillside Avenue (Abertridwr)
...............................**40** E5
Hillside Avenue (Llanharan)
...............................**17** D5
Hillside Close **22** G6
Hillside Court...........**33** B2/**36** H1
Hillside Street **8** H3
Hillside Terrace (Bedwas) ..**42** H1
Hillside Terrace (Gelli) **9** B6
Hillside Terrace (Pontypridd)
...............................**32** E1
Hillside Terrace (Tonypandy)
...............................**11** A6
Hillside Terrace (Wattstown)
...............................**12** F4
Hillside View (Ferndale)...**10** F4
Hillside View (Pontypridd) .**31** D1
Hilltop Avenue **30** H6
Hilltop Close **27** A4
Hilltop Cottages **31** D6
Hilltop Crescent **32** G2
Hillview Terrace..................**24** H2
Hiraethog Road **39** C4
Hirwain Terrace **19** C5
Hirwaun Place **12** E1
Hirwaun Road (Aberdare)
...........................**2** H6/**3** B2
Hirwaun Road (Hirwaun)
..........................**1** C3/**2** F5
Hoddinotts Houses **9** A4
Hodges Street **19** D4
Holborn Terrace................**13** B2
Holbrook Close **8** F2
Holford Street (Aberdare) **4** E5
Holford Terrace **2** F6
Hollies Cottages **28** E6
Hollies, The (Pontyclun) **17** A3
Hollies, The (Quaker's Yard)
...............................**27** B4
Hollies,The (Heolgerrig)...**18** F1
Holly Lane **32** G1
Holly Road **15** B6
Holly Row **23** D6
Holly Street (Gilfach Goch) **15** A5
Holly Street (Rhydyfelin) ...**39** A2
Holly Terrace.....................**22** G2
Holly Way **19** C3
Hollybush Close **34** H4
Hollybush Estate **37** D5
Hollybush Grove **29** A4
Hollybush Terrace **34** H4
Hollybush Villas **34** H4
Holmwood...............**33** A2/**36** H1
Holy Drive **2** F6
Holyhead Court **41** A4
Holyrood Terrace **11** A5
Holywell Road **39** A5
Homerton Street **25** D1
Honeysuckle Close **19** A3
Honiton Cottages **14** E2
Hopkin Street......................**7** D6
Hopkins Close **21** C6
Hopkinstown Road **31** C1
Horeb Close **19** D5
Horeb Street (M. Tydfil) **18** E2
Horeb Street (Treorchy) **8** G2
Horeb Terrace.....................**2** H2
Hornbeam Close **19** B2
Horner Row **9** B1
Horse Cottages **1** D3

Hospital Flats.......................**3** D2
Hospital Road **32** G2
Houlson Road **20** F3
Howard Drive.....................**41** D2
Howard Street (Clydach Vale)
...............................**12** F2
Howard Street (Treorchy) **8** F3
Howell Close............**18** G1/**19** B6
Howell Street.....................**30** H4
Howells Row (Aberaman) **5** D1
Howells Row (Cwmdare)......**2** E6
Hughes Street (Mt. Ash) **23** C5
Hughes Street (Tonypandy)
...............................**13** B2
Hunt Terrace **18** H4
Hurford Crescent **31** D2
Hurford Street **31** D2
Hurst Grove **3** D2
Hyland Place **1** B1
Hylton Terrace...................**28** G5

I

Idloes Place **12** E1
Iestyn Street **2** G5/**3** A1
Ifor Place **27** A3
Ifor Street..........................**23** C3
Ilan Avenue **32** H5
Ilan Road **40** F6
Illtyd Street (Pontypridd) ...**31** D4
Illtyd Street (Treorchy) **8** F3
Imperial Court **26** G5
Incline Cottages................**11** B6
Incline Road **4** G4
Incline Row (Aberdare) **5** D2
Incline Row (Ynyshir) **12** G5
Incline Side **21** D1
Incline Top (Abercynon) ...**26** H3
Incline Top (M. Tydfil) **20** E6
Industrial Terrace **22** G2
Insole Terrace **35** C4
Institute Place **11** B6
Institute Road **11** A6
Institute Street **9** A1
Inverleith Terrace...............**11** A6
Investiture Place **16** H3
Irene Street **23** C5
Irfon Terrace **10** F5
Iron Bridge Road **37** B3
Ironworks Road **1** B1
Islwyn Drive **41** D3
Islwyn Terrace **14** F2
Isycoed **9** B3
Ivor Park **17** A3
Ivor Street (Dowlais) **20** F4
Ivor Street (Trehafod) **29** C5
Ivor Street (Ystrad) **9** C6
Ivor Terrace **20** E3
Ivy Close **19** C4
Ivy Cottages*, Main Road .**38** E4
Ivy Terrace **31** C1

J

James Place **32** G4
James Street (Aberdare) **2** E6
James Street (Maerdy) **9** A1
James Street (M. Tydfil) **21** B1
James Street (Mt. Ash) **23** C5
James Street (Tonypandy) **13** C3
James Street (Treforest) ...**32** G5
James Street (Treorchy) **8** G3
James Street (Trethomas)..**43** B1
James Terrace (Llantrisant)
...............................**36** F4

James Terrace (Tonypandy)
...............................**13** C3
James Terrace (Ynyshir)...**14** G1
Janet Street **32** H6
Japonica Drive **20** G4
Jasmine Close **19** A3
Jeffrey Street **23** C2
Jenkin Houses **21** C6
Jenkin Street (Abercwmboi)
.............................**6** F2/G3
Jenkin Street (Aberdare) **3** C4
Jenkin Street (Porth) **14** H4
Jenkins Place **21** B1
Jenkins Row*, High St. **21** C6
Jenkins Street (Abercynon) **26** H4
Jenkins Street (Pontypridd) **31** D1
Jenner Walk **34** G4
Jerrys Lane **42** G2
Jesmondene **38** G5
Jestyn Street **14** G2
Jobs Lane **18** G4
John Place **32** G5
John Street (Abercwmboi) ...**6** F2
John Street (Aberdare) **3** C4
John Street (Hirwaun) **1** B1
John Street (M. Tydfil) **21** A1
John Street (Mt. Ash) **23** D4
John Street (Pentre) **8** H4
John Street (Porth) **14** H3
John Street (Treforest) **32** G5
John Street (Treharris) **27** B3
John Street (Treherbert) **7** D5
John Street (Ynyshir).........**12** H6
Johnson Park......................**1** B3
Jonathans Terrace **30** H4
Jones Court **19** B6
Jones Place **32** G1
Jones Street (Blaen Clydach)
...............................**12** G2
Jones Street (Cilfynydd) **30** H3
Jones Street (M. Tydfil) **20** F2
Jones Street (Mt. Ash).......**23** C5
Jones Street (Treorchy).......**7** D6
Jones Terrace (M. Tydfil)...**21** B1
Jones Terrace*, Horeb St...**18** E2
Jowett Avenue **21** C2
Jubilee Court **12** E2
Jubilee Road **4** E6
Jubilee Street **17** D6
Julians Close **28** H2
Junction Terrace **37** C6
Justin Lane **23** C4

K

Keble Court **43** D1
Keir Hardie Housing Estate
...............................**21** C2
Keith Street **12** E1
Kendal Close **4** F4
Kendon Court **1** A2
Kennard Street **8** H6/**9** A6
Kennedy Close **33** D6
Kenry Street (Evanstown) ..**15** A2
Kenry Street (Tonypandy) .**13** A1
Kenry Street (Treorchy) **7** D6
Kensington Drive **29** A5
Kents Court **21** B5
Kenwyn Terrace.................**30** F6
Kerslake Terrace **13** B3
Kevin Ryan Court*,
    Heol S. O. Davies **18** G1
Kidwelly Court **41** A3
Kidwelly Grove..................**18** E6

Kiln Street **4** E5
Kimberley Place*, Merthyr Rd.
...............................**22** G2
Kimberley Way **14** H4
King Close*, King Street **40** F5
King Edward Avenue **42** E6
King Edward Street **19** C5
King Street (Aberaman) **4** E5
King Street (Abercynon) ...**26** H4
King Street (Aberdare).........**2** G2
King Street (Abertridwr) **40** F5
King Street (Ferndale) **10** F5
King Street (Gelli) **9** A6
King Street (M. Tydfil) **20** E1
King Street (Miskin) **23** C5
King Street (Taff's Well) **38** G6
King Street (Treforest).......**32** G4
Kingcraft Street **23** B4
Kings Avenue **37** C6
Kings Road **37** B6
Kingsacre **33** A2/**36** H1
Kingsbury Court...................**2** H3
Kingsbury Place (Cwmaman)
.................................**5** B3
Kingsbury Place (Llwydcoed)
.................................**2** H3
Kingsland Terrace **32** G4
Kingsley Place **40** E2
Kingsley Terrace (Aberfan) **24** G2
Kingsley Terrace (M. Tydfil) ......
...............................**21** B1
Kirkhouse Street **32** E3
Knight Street **23** B3
Knight Terrace **26** H4
Knoll Cottages **11** A5
Knoll Terrace...........**11** A6/**12** H2

L

Laburnum Lane **18** H2
Laburnam Terrace (Troedyrhiw)
...............................**22** F2
Laburnum Close **19** C4
Laburnum Court................**39** B2
Laburnum Drive...................**2** G6
Laburnum Terrace (Rhydyfelin)
...............................**39** A2
Ladysmith Place*, Merthyr Rd.
...............................**22** G2
Lake Street **10** F4
Lakeside Gardens **18** H3
Lakeside*, Hazel Drive **1** A4
Lamb Road **1** A4
Lambert Terrace **3** B3
Lan Close **32** E1
Lan Park Road...................**32** E1
Lan Wood Road **31** D1
Lan y Parc **1** A2
Lancaster Drive **33** B1/**34** F6
Lancaster Street **19** B6
Lancaster Villas*, Lancaster St.
...............................**19** B6
Lanelay Close **35** A5
Lanelay Cottages...............**35** A5
Lanelay Crescent **31** D2
Lanelay Park **35** A5
Lanelay Road **35** A5
Lanelay Terrace **31** D2
Langland Close **1** A2
Lansbury Close **41** C2
Lansbury Road **18** G5
Lansdale Drive **39** A6
Lanwern Road **31** D3
Larch Close **19** B3

Larch Court 37 C2
Larch Drive 36 E4
Larch Grove 42 F2
Larch House 37 D5
Larch Wood 15 D5
Larkfield Avenue 4 F4
Laundry Road 31 D2
Laura Street 32 F3
Laurel Avenue 39 B3
Laurel Close 2 G6
Laurel Court....................42 H1
Laureldene......................15 A6
Laurels, The 17 D5
Laurels, The*, Cardiff Rd. ..23 C3
Lavender Road 19 A3
Lawn Terrace (Treforest) ..32 G4
Lawn Terrace*, Bethesda Street
....19 B6
Lawrence Avenue 1 D3
Lawrence Street 42 E4
Lee Street 31 D2
Legions Way 28 G2
Leigh Terrace 27 A4
Leighton Rees Close 25 B6
Leon Avenue 38 G6
Leslie Terrace 14 H3/29 A4
Lewis Arms Row 13 D5
Lewis Drive 41 D2
Lewis Place 14 G4
Lewis Square 21 A5
Lewis Street (Aberdare) 4 E5
Lewis Street (Bedlinog) 28 H5
Lewis Street (Church Village)
....34 H4
Lewis Street (Machen) 43 C5
Lewis Street (Mt. Ash) 23 C2
Lewis Street (Pentre)...........8 H4
Lewis Street (Pontyclun) 17 B1
Lewis Street (Pontypridd) ..32 E3
Lewis Street (Tonypandy) ..13 C3
Lewis Street (Treforest)......32 G4
Lewis Street (Trehafod)......29 C5
Lewis Terrace (Heolgerrig) 18 F1
Lewis Terrace (M. Tydfil) 19 D5
Lewis Terrace (Pontypridd) 32 F1
Lewis Terrace (Porth) 29 A4
Lewis Terrace (Wattstown) 12 F4
Leyshon Close 38 F5
Leyshon Street 31 D4
Leyshon Terrace 29 A5
Libanus Street 20 E3
Library Close (Pentre) 9 A5
Library Close (Pontypridd) .39 A2
Library Lane 21 B1
Library Road (Pontypridd) ..32 E2
Library Road (Tonypandy) ..13 C3
Lilac Drive 36 H1
Lime Grove 19 C4
Lime Street (Ferndale).......10 F4
Lime Street (Rhydyfelin) 39 A2
Limeslade Close 1 A2
Limetree Close 34 G5
Lincoln Street 14 G4
Linden Court 15 A6
Linden Crescent 3 A3
Linden Grove 42 F2
Linden Way 19 A1
Lionel Terrace 32 H6
Lisburn Rise......................1 B1
Lister Close 34 F4
Little Row.........................3 D1
Little Wind Street 3 C4
Littlewoods Estate 26 F6

Llan Rhyd.........................22 F3
Llan Ty Gwyn 40 G5
Llanarth Close*, Llanarth Street
....43 D5
Llanarth Street.................43 D5
Llanbad 17 A5
Llanberis Close 34 G3
Llanbradach Street 32 E2
Llanbryn Gardens 17 C4
Llancaiach Cottages 28 E3
Llancaiach Court 27 D4
Llancaiach View 27 D5
Llandaff Way 14 G6
Llanddewi Street 4 E6
Llandraw Bungalows 31 C3
Llandraw Court 31 C2
Llandraw Road 31 C2
Llandraw Woods 31 C2
Llanerch Goed 34 F4
Llanfabon Court 30 H6
Llanfabon Drive........42 H1/43 A1
Llanfabon Road 27 C6
Llanfair Hill 9 A6
Llanfair Road (Pontypridd) 31 D3
Llanfair Road (Tonypandy) 13 C3
Llanfedw Close 42 G2
Llanfoist Street..................9 A5
Llangorse Road 4 F4/G4
Llanharry Road 17 A3
Llanover Road 32 F1
Llanrhyd*, Diana Street 22 F3
Llantrisant Houses............35 D4
Llantrisant Road (Beddau)
.........................33 B6/36 E2
Llantrisant Road (Church Village)
....34 E6
Llantrisant Road (Llan. Fardre)
...................33 A2/34 E6
Llantrisant Road
(Pen-y-coedcae) 33 C1
Llantrisant Road (Pontyclun)
....17 B1
Llantrisant Road (Pontypridd)
....31 C6
Llantrisant Road (Tonyrefail)
....16 G1
Llantwit Road 32 G6/39 A4
Llanwonno Close 31 C1
Llanwonno Road (Cwmaman)
....5 B3
Llanwonno Road (Mt. Ash)
....23 B4
Llanwonno Road (Pontypridd)
....31 C1
Llanwonno Road (Stanleytown)
....12 E3
Llanwonno Road (Ynyshir)
...................12 H6/14 H1
Lle Hyfryd 2 G3
Llest Cottages 33 A2/34 E6
Llest Terrace 33 A2/34 E6
Lletecca Place 9 A4
Llewellyn Drive 41 D3
Llewellyn Place*, Llewellyn St.
....9 A4
Llewellyn Street (Blaencwm) 7 A6
Llewellyn Street (Dowlais) ..20 E2
Llewellyn Street (Gilfach Goch)
....15 B5
Llewellyn Street (M. Tydfil)
....19 B5
Llewellyn Street (Pentre)
.........................8 H4/9 A4

Llewellyn Street (Pontypridd)
....31 C1
Llewellyn Street (Tonypandy)
....13 B2
Llewellyn Street (Treherbert) 7 D6
Llewellyn Street (Tylorstown)
....12 E3
Llewellyn Terrace (Llwynypia)
....11 A6
Llewellyn Terrace (Trealaw)
....13 D2
Llewellyn Terrace (Ynysybwl)
....25 B6
Llewelyn Court....................3 A1
Llewelyn Street (Aberdare)
......................2 G5/3 A1
Lloyd Street 9 A6
Lloyds Court*, Lloyds Ter...19 D5
Lloyds Terrace.................19 D5
Llwyd y Berth 41 B5
Llwydcoed Road 2 H4
Llwyfen Street 19 B6
Llwyn Bedw 6 H1
Llwyn Berry 19 B6
Llwyn Brynmelin 19 B6
Llwyn Derw 11 B6
Llwyn Dic Penderyn 18 G1/19 B6
Llwyn Drysgol 37 A5
Llwyn Eithin 42 G3
Llwyn Gwyn 15 A6
Llwyn Mallt......................37 C3
Llwyn On Close 41 C3
Llwyn On Street...............41 C3
Llwyn Onn (Penderyn).........1 A6
Llwyn Onn (Pontyclun) 17 A1
Llwyn Onn Cottages 34 G3
Llwyn Pennau Cottages.....36 F6
Llwyn yr Eos (Abercanaid)..21 B5
Llwyn yr Eos (M. Tydfil) 19 D6
Llwyn yr Eos (Nelson) 27 D5
Llwynbrain Terrace 17 D4
Llwyncelyn Close 18 G2
Llwyncelyn Cottages (M. Tydfil)
....18 G4
Llwyncelyn Cottages
(Merthyr Vale) 24 H2
Llwyncelyn Court 29 A4
Llwyncelyn Parc 29 A4
Llwyncelyn Road 29 A5
Llwyncelyn Terrace 27 C6
Llwyncrwn Road 33 C6
Llwynderi 2 E3
Llwynfen Road.................17 B2
Llwyngoleu Cottages........28 G1
Llwynmadoc Street 32 E2
Llwynycelyn Lane 18 G2
Llwynypia Cottages 37 A4
Llwynypia Road 11 B5/B6
Llwynypia Terrace 11 B5
Llyn Crescent 10 E5
Llyn Pandy 42 G1
Llys Alaw 13 D1
Llys Ben Bowen Thomas
.....................9 C5/11 A2
Llys Bryn Felin 16 F3
Llys Canaid 21 C5
Llys Caradog 36 H6
Llys Catwg 35 B5
Llys Celyn 39 A6
Llys Coed 30 F3
Llys Coed Derw 34 F5
Llys Corrwg 39 B2
Llys Cynon 1 C2

Llys Deri..........................15 B6
Llys Derwen (Coed y Cwm) 30 F3
Llys Derwen (Llantrisant)....35 C5
Llys Dewi 36 H6
Llys Dyfodwg (Creigiau) ...36 H6
Llys Dyfodwg (Talbot Grn.) 35 B5
Llys Dyfrig 36 H6
Llys Fach 34 H5
Llys Garth 34 F4
Llys Glanrhondda 8 H3
Llys Gwilym 29 C1
Llys Gwynno 36 H6
Llys Hafen 38 G6
Llys Hebron 9 A5
Llys Illtyd (Creigiau).........36 H6
Llys Illtyd (Talbot Grn.) 35 B5
Llys Joseph 15 B6
Llys Llywelyn 34 F5
Llys Maelwg 35 B5
Llys Maendy 9 A5
Llys Nant Glas 24 E6
Llys Nant Pandy 41 D4
Llys Nant yr Aber.............41 D4
Llys Nazareth 8 H4
Llys Scimitar 38 F6
Llys Siloh 9 A4
Llys Teilo (Creigiau) 36 H6
Llys Teilo (Talbot Grn.) 35 B5
Llys Treherbert 29 D3
Llys Tripp 38 F6
Llys Tudful 36 H6
Llys Ty Gwyn...................32 G1
Llys Tylcha Fawr..............16 G3
Llys y Celyn 42 F2
Llys y Fedwen 42 F3
Llys y Fran......................34 G5
Llys yr Efail 16 G3
Llys yr Onnen 23 C3
Llyswen (Machen) 43 B5
Llyswen (Penywaun) 2 E4
Lock Street 26 H4
Lon Elai 17 B1
Lon Fach 41 C5
Lon Fawr........................41 C5
Lon Hafren......................41 C6
Lon Helygen....................30 F3
Lon Heulog 39 A3
Lon Isaf 41 C5
Lon Las 2 G3
Lon Robin Coch...............41 B5
Lon Uchaf 41 C5
Lon y Felin 23 A1
Lon y Barri 41 C2
Lon y Brynnau 2 F6
Lon y Cadno 34 G5
Lon y Celyn 27 D5
Lon y Dderwen 27 D5
Lon y Ddraenen 41 C5
Lon y Deri 41 C5
Lon y Fran......................41 B4
Lon y Garwa 41 C6
Lon y Gors......................41 C5
Lon y Llwyn 27 D5
Lon y Llyn 41 C5
Lon y Rhedyn 41 C5
Lon y Tresglen 41 B4
Lon y Twyn 42 E5
Lon y Waun 41 C5
Lon y Wern 41 C5
Lon yr Awel 17 C1
Lon yr Odyn 42 F5
Lon yr Ysgol 42 G1
London Street 23 C2

Long Acre Close 35 D4
Long Row............................10 F3
Longfellow Gardens 43 D1
Longfield Court 1 B2
Longmede Park...................1 D5
Longwood Drive.................37 B5
Lord Street............................4 E5
Low Row 23 A1
Lower Alma Place 9 A4
Lower Bailey Street 12 G4
Lower Brynhyfryd Terrace ..40 F2
Lower Cross Street 1 A2
Lower Dunraven Street*,
    Gelli Road.....................13 B1
Lower Edward Street (4) 19 B6
Lower Forest Level 23 D3
Lower Francis Street 40 F5
Lower Glyn Gwyn Street ...43 B2
Lower High Street 21 A2
Lower Mount Pleasant 22 G3
Lower Rhymney Valley
    Relief Road 41 D1
Lower Row..........................20 F3
Lower Station Street 4 F6
Lower Street 4 F6
Lower Taff View 30 G6
Lower Terrace (Stanleytown)
    ....12 E2
Lower Terrace (Treorchy) 8 E4
Lower Thomas Street 21 A1
Lower Union Street 20 F4
Lower Vaynor Road...........18 H3
Lowerdale Drive 35 D5
Lowlands Drive 39 A6
Ludlow Street 41 D5
Lupin Close 19 A3
Luther Lane 21 C1
Luther Street 21 C1
Luton Street (Blaenllechau) 10 F3
Luton Street (Treorchy) 8 F2
Lydwood Close 43 C5
Lyle Street 23 B3
Lyndhurst Street 23 B2
Lynwood Court 37 B6

M

Mace Lane...........................8 E1
Mackintosh Road 32 F2
Mackintosh Street 22 G6
Mackintosh Terrace...........27 D3
Maddox Street 12 H2
Madeline Street (Pentre) 8 H4
Madeline Street (Pontygwaith)
    ....12 E3
Madison Drive 1 B2
Madoc Street 32 E3
Madog Close 10 G6
Maelgwyn Terrace 3 B3
Maelog Close 17 B1
Maen Ganol.......................27 D1
Maen Gilfach 27 D1
Maendy Crescent 18 H5
Maendy Place*, Canon St. ..3 C3
Maendy Road 31 D5
Maerdy Cottages 9 A2
Maerdy Court.......................9 A2
Maerdy Road Flats 9 A2
Maerdy Road (Aberdare) 3 A5/A6
Maerdy Road (Maerdy) 9 A2
Maes Bedw 14 H5
Maes Briallu 42 G3
Maes Brynna 2 F6
Maes Cadwgan 36 H6

Maes Cefn Mably 35 D3
Maes Draenog....................37 C1
Maes Ganol 39 B3
Maes Glas (Caerphilly) 42 F5
Maes Glas (Coed y Cwm) ..30 F3
Maes Glas Cottages*, Main Rd.
    ....38 E4
Maes Gwyn (Caerphilly) 42 E5
Maes Gwyn (Porth) 14 H4
Maes Hir 41 C2
Maes Maelwg 36 E1
Maes Mafon Cottages 27 D5
Maes Melyn 2 F6
Maes Meyrick*, Heol Gerrig18 E2
Maes Rhydwen 2 H5/3 A1
Maes Sarn 35 D3
Maes Trane 36 F1
Maes Trisant 35 B5
Maes Uchaf 29 C3
Maes Watford*,
    Heol Waun Waelod 41 C6
Maes y Awel 37 A5
Maes y Bedw 28 G5
Maes y Briallu 37 A4
Maes y Bryn (Cardiff).........37 A4
Maes y Bryn (Tonyrefail) ...16 G2
Maes y Coed (Aberdare) 2 F6
Maes y Coed (Nelson)........27 D3
Maes y Cored 37 D6
Maes y Dderwen 36 H6
Maes y Deri (Aberdare) 6 E1
Maes y Deri (Pontypridd)....36 H6
Maes y Drudwen 41 B5
Maes y Felin (Caerphilly) ...42 E4
Maes y Felin (Rhydyfelin) ...39 B3
Maes y Felin Crescent 17 B2
Maes y Ffynon 20 F4
Maes y Fioled 37 A4
Maes y Gollen 36 H6
Maes y Grub 34 G4
Maes y Nant 36 H6
Maes y Pandy 42 F1
Maes y Rhedyn (Creigiau)..36 H6
Maes y Rhedyn (Maerdy) 9 B3
Maes y Rhedyn (Talbot Grn.)
    ....35 B4
Maes y Siglen 41 B4
Maes y Wennol 17 D1
Maes yr Afon (Caerphilly) ..42 G2
Maes yr Afon (Pontyclun) ..17 B2
Maes yr Awel 39 B3
Maes yr Eglwys..................34 G3
Maes yr Haf (Llwydcoed).....2 H4
Maes yr Haf (M. Tydfil) 21 B1
Maes yr Hafod 36 H6
Maes yr Haul Cottages 35 D5
Maes yr Helig 2 H3
Maes yr Onen (Nelson) 27 D5
Maes yr Onnen (Creigiau)..36 H6
Maescynon....................1 B1/C2
Maesgwyn (Aberdare) 2 F5
Maesgwynne (M. Tydfil) 18 H5
Maeshyfryd 4 G6
Maestaf Street 21 D6
Maesteg Crescent 39 A6
Maesteg Gardens 39 A6
Maesteg Grove 39 A6
Maesycoed Road 31 D2
Maesycoed Villas 9 D6/11 A2
Maesyffynon Grove 3 D5
Maesyffynon Lane 3 C5
Maesyffynon Terrace..........13 C1

Maesygarreg 18 G4
Mafon Cottages 27 A5
Mafon Road.......................27 A5
Magnolia Close (M. Tydfil)..19 C3
Magnolia Close (Porth) 29 A4
Magnolia Way 36 H1
Main Avenue 39 D5
Main Road (Abercynon) 25 D1
Main Road (Church Village)
    ....34 H4/39 A6
Main Road (Cross Inn) 36 E4
Main Road (Morganstown) 37 A3
Main Road (Taff's Well)
    ....37 A1/38 E2/E3
Maindy Court.....................34 G3
Maindy Crescent 8 H5
Maindy Croft 8 H5
Maindy Grove 8 H5
Maindy Road..............8 H5/9 A5
Malus Avenue 36 H1
Manchester Place 1 A2
Mandeg 27 D3
Mangoed 1 D3
Manley Close 16 G3
Manobier Close 34 H3
Manor Chase 36 F2
Manor Court 34 G4
Manor Hill 17 B2
Manor Park 17 A6
Manorau*, Queens Road....21 B1
Mansfield Terrace 21 C1
Maple Close (Llanharry) 15 A6
Maple Close (M. Tydfil) 19 C4
Maple Court 16 H3
Maple Crescent 19 A2
Maple Drive 3 A3
Maple Street 39 A2
Maple Terrace 6 F3
Mardy Close (Caerphilly) ...42 F4
Mardy Close (M. Tydfil) 21 B2
Mardy Crescent 42 F4
Mardy Street 21 C1
Mardy Terrace 21 B3
Margaret Street (Aberaman) 6 E1
Margaret Street (Abercwmboi)
    ....6 G3
Margaret Street (Abercynon)
    ....26 G5
Margaret Street (Aberdare)
    ....2 H6/3 B1
Margaret Street (5) (M. Tydfil)
    ....19 B5
Margaret Street (Pentre) 8 H3
Margaret Street (Pontygwaith)
    ....12 E4
Margaret Street (Pontypridd)
    ....31 C1
Margaret Street (Trehafod) 29 C5
Margaret Street (Treherbert) 7 B4
Marian Street 12 F2
Marigold Close...................19 A3
Maritime Court*, Greenway 42 F1
Maritime Street 31 D3
Maritime Terrace 31 D3
Marjorie Street...................13 D2
Market Square 21 A1
Market Street (Aberdare).......3 C3
Market Street (Caerphilly) ..42 E5
Market Street (Dowlais) 20 F4
Market Street (Pontypridd) 32 E2
Market Street (Tongwynlais)
    ....37 B2
Marlais Buildings*, High St. 19 C6

Marlborough Close ..33 B2/34 F6
Marshall Crescent 19 D3
Marsham Court 37 B6
Marshfield Court 16 H3
Marshfield Road 9 C3
Martin Close......................18 F1
Martin Crescent 16 G3
Martins Lane 26 G5
Martins Terrace 26 G5
Mary Ann Street.................20 E3
Mary Street (Abercwmboi) ...6 F3
Mary Street (Aberdare) 3 C4
Mary Street (Bedlinog) 28 H5
Mary Street (Cilfynydd) 30 H4
Mary Street (M. Tydfil) 21 B2
Mary Street (Mt. Ash) 23 D4
Mary Street (Porth) 14 H2
Mary Street (Treharris) 27 A3
Mary Street (Treherbert) 7 D6
Mary Street (Trethomas) 43 B2
Mary Street*, Upper Elizabeth St.
    ....20 E4
Masefield Way 39 A1
Mason Street (Abercwmboi) 6 F3
Mason Street (Aberdare) 4 E6
Masonic Street...................21 A1
Matexa Street 8 H6
Matthews Terrace 33 C1
Mattie Collins Way 8 F4
Maxton Court 42 F4
Maxwell Street 10 F4
Mayfield Place 35 D4
Mayfield Road 31 D1
Mayors Square 18 E2
Maywood 17 B5
Meadow Brook 34 H5
Meadow Close (Hirwaun) 1 C2
Meadow Close (Llanharan) 17 C4
Meadow Close (Mt. Ash) 23 A2
Meadow Close (Tonyrefail) 16 E5
Meadow Court 21 B3
Meadow Crescent
    (Caerphilly).................42 E5
Meadow Crescent
    (Church Village) 39 A6
Meadow Hill 34 H4
Meadow Lane (Gilfach Goch)
    ....15 A4
Meadow Lane (Hirwaun) 1 A2
Meadow Rise 17 B4/C4
Meadow Street (Gilfach Goch)
    ....15 A4
Meadow Street (Treforest) 32 G5
Meadow View 42 F1
Meadow Walk 9 B5
Meadow Way 41 B6
Meadowbank Close 4 F4
Medway Court 33 B1/34 F6
Meirion Place*, Heol Gerrig 18 F1
Meirion Street (Aberdare)
    ....2 H6/3 B2
Meirion Street (Tonypandy) 13 C3
Meiros Close 17 C6
Melbourne Buildings*, John St.
    ....6 F2
Melbourne Terrace 17 A1
Melin Caiach 27 B3
Mellte Villas 2 H3
Melville Terrace 42 E3
Menai Close 34 G3
Menelaus Square*, Victoria St.
    ....20 E3
Merchant Street...................3 D3

Merlin Gwlan 41 C3
Merthyr Road (Aberdare) 2 G3
Merthyr Road (Hirwaun) 1 B2
Merthyr Road (M. Tydfil) 19 D5
Merthyr Road (Pentrebach)
 ....21 B4/C6/22 F1
Merthyr Road (Pontypridd) 32 F2
Merthyr Road (Tongwynlais)
 ....37 B2
Merthyr Street 17 B1
Mervyn Street (Aberfan) 22 G6
Mervyn Street (Rhydyfelin) 32 H6
Mews, The*, Church St. ...35 C3
Meyler Street 16 F6
Meyrick Villas...................19 B5
Meyricks Row 13 C5
Michaels Road....................7 A6
Mid Rhondda Access.........13 A1
Middle Row (Blaenllechau) 10 F3
Middle Row (Mt. Ash) 23 A1
Middle Row*, Middle St. 13 C2
Middle Street (Pontypridd) .32 F1
Middle Street (Tonypandy) 13 C2
Middle Terrace.................12 E2
Mikado Street 13 B2
Milbourne Close................21 B3
Milbourne Street (Abercynon)
 ....25 D1
Milbourne Street (Tonypandy)
 ....13 D3
Milbourne Terrace 21 B3
Mildred Close 33 C6
Mildred Street 33 D5
Miles Court.......................38 F6
Miles Street (Maerdy) 9 A2
Miles Street (6) (M. Tydfil) .19 B5
Milford Close 34 H3
Mill Close.........................41 C3
Mill Lane (Llanharan).........17 D5
Mill Lane (M. Tydfil)...........19 D5
Mill Place 23 A1
Mill Race 17 D3
Mill Road (Caerphilly) 41 D3
Mill Road (Mt. Ash) 23 A1
Mill Road (Tongwynlais) 37 B2
Mill Road (Ynysybwl) 25 B5
Mill Street (Aberdare) ...2 H6/3 A1
Mill Street (Pontypridd) 32 E2
Mill Street (Tonyrefail) 16 F4
Mill Street (Treharris)........27 B3
Mill Street (Ystrad) 9 D6/11 A2
Mill Terrace......................27 A5
Millers Row 27 A4
Millfield (Pontyclun) 17 A2
Millfield (Treharris)............27 C3
Milton Close 36 F1
Milton Place (Trethomas) ..43 D1
Milton Place*, Court Ter. ...21 B1
Milton Street 5 B3
Milton Terrace*, Court Ter. 21 B1
Min y Coed 37 A4
Min yr Afon 43 C5
Miners Row 2 H3
Miskin Cottages*, Miskin Road
 ....23 C4
Miskin Crescent................17 D2
Miskin Road (Miskin)..........17 D2
Miskin Road (Mt. Ash)........23 C3
Miskin Road (Tonypandy)
 ....11 B6/13 B1
Miskin Street 7 B4
Miskin Terrace...................23 C4
Mitchell Court....................11 A6

Mitchell Crescent.*...........19 D3
Mitchells Terrace 32 F3
Modern Cottages 19 D6
Moel Fryn..........................41 A2
Moir Court 41 C2
Mona Place 9 A1
Monk Street........................3 C4
Monmouth Close 34 H3
Monmouth Court 41 B3
Monmouth Drive 18 F5
Monmouth Street...............25 C1
Montana Caravan Park 1 C3
Monumental Terrace*,
 New Church Street ...18 G3
Moorland Close 1 C2
Moorland Crescent 33 D6
Moorland Heights 32 G3
Morgan Court....................11 B4
Morgan Row 4 G5
Morgan Jones Maisonettes 41 D4
Morgan Jones Square........22 G3
Morgan Street (Aberdare) 3 B3
Morgan Street (Caerphilly) 41 D3
Morgan Street (M. Tydfil)....19 B6
Morgan Street (Mt. Ash) 23 C5
Morgan Street (Pontypridd) 32 E1
Morgan Street (Porth) 14 H4
Morgan Street*, North St. ..20 E4
Morgan Terrace (Porth)......14 H4
Morgan Terrace (Treorchy) ..8 E4
Morgannwg Street 29 C5
Morgannwg Terrace*, Cardiff Rd.
 ....24 H2
Moriah Place 2 H3
Moriah Street (Bedlinog) ...28 G5
Moriah Street (5) (M. Tydfil)19 B6
Morien Crescent 32 H4/H5
Morlais Buildings*, High St.19 C6
Morlais Close 18 F5
Morlais Court....................41 A3
Morlais Street (Dowlais) 20 E3
Morlais Street (M. Tydfil) ...21 D6
Morrell Street....................21 B1
Morris Avenue 24 E6
Morris Street (Cwmaman) ...5 B3
Morris Street (Treherbert) ...7 D6
Morris Terrace 10 E3
Morton Terrace 12 F2
Moss Place 3 D1
Moss Row 3 D1
Mostyn Close 17 A5
Mostyn Mews*, Mostyn Cl. 17 A5
Mostyn Street 6 G3
Mound Road 31 D3
Mount Hill Street 4 E6
Mount Libanus Street 7 D5
Mount Pleasant (Bedlinog) 28 H5
Mount Pleasant (Heolgerrig)
 ....18 F1
Mount Pleasant (Merthyr Vale)
 ....24 H4
Mount Pleasant (Trehafod) 29 B5
Mount Pleasant Cottages*,
 Victoria Street 23 C4
Mount Pleasant Place 23 C5
Mount Pleasant Road 14 G2
Mount Pleasant Street
 (Aberdare) 2 E6/3 B1/B2
Mount Pleasant Street (Dowlais)
 ....20 E3
Mount Pleasant Terrace 23 C4
Mount Street (Aberdare) 4 E6
Mount Street (M. Tydfil) 19 B6

Mount Terrace (7) 19 B5
Mount View (M. Tydfil).......21 D1
Mount View (Merthyr Vale) 24 H4
Mount View Estate 21 D1
Mount View Flats...............32 H5
Mountain Road 42 G1
Mountain Ash Road...........26 F5
Mountain Hare Cottages*,
 Mount View 21 D1
Mountain Road (Caerphilly)42 E5
Mountain Road (Cwmaman) 5 B3
Mountain Road (Williamstown)
 ....13 C4
Mountain Row 10 E2
Mountain View (Abertridwr) 40 H5
Mountain View (Caerphilly) 41 D1
Mountain View (Machen)....43 B5
Mountain View (Tonypandy)
 ....11 C4
Mountain View (Tonyrefail) 15 D6
Mountain View (Treherbert)..7 B4
Mountain Way 28 E6
Moy Road (Aberfan) 22 G6
Moy Road (Taff's Well) 38 F5
Mr. Speakers Way.............13 C2
Mulberry Close 36 H1
Muriel Terrace (Bedlinog) ..28 H6
Muriel Terrace (Dowlais) ...20 F3
Murrells Close 33 B2/36 H1
Mwyndy Terrace 36 E6
Mynachdy Road................25 A5
Mynydd y Seren................16 E5
Mynydd yr Eos..................13 C3
Myrtle Row 8 H3

N

Nant Caiach.....................28 E5
Nant Celyn.........................1 A2
Nant Ddu 41 D5
Nant Dyfed 36 E2
Nant Eirin 16 E4
Nant Gwyddon Close 9 C6
Nant Gwyn (Aberdare).........2 F5
Nant Gwyn (Trelewis) 27 D3
Nant Melyn Terrace...........16 H6
Nant Morlais.....................20 F2
Nant y Coed (Thomastown)16 E5
Nant y Coed (Troedyrhiw) ..22 F3
Nant y Dwrgi 17 D5
Nant y Fedw 26 E2
Nant y Felin 34 E2
Nant y Garth 38 F6
Nant y Gwyddon Road
 ....9 B6/11 A3
Nant y Hwyad 41 B4
Nant y Mynydd..................30 F2
Nant yr Arian 34 G3
Nantddu Terrace 26 H1
Nantgarw Road 41 B6/C5
Nantgwyn (Porth)..............14 F5
Nantgwyn (Trelewis) 27 D3
Nantgwyn Street 13 B2
Nantydall Avenue 34 H1
Nantygwenith Street 18 G1/19 B6
Napier Street (Machen)......43 C5
Napier Street (Mt. Ash) 23 C3
Narberth Court..................41 A3
Nash Street 26 F5
Naval Yard........................13 C2
Navigation Close 27 B2
Navigation Street (Mt. Ash) 23 C3
Navigation Street (Trethomas)
 ....43 A1

Navigation Villas 23 C4
Navigation Yard.................23 C3
Nebo Estate.......................9 C6
Nelson Street......................5 C2
Neol Street 5 C2
Neville Terrace 3 B3
New Blandy Terrace 15 B1
New Bryn Terrace 12 F4
New Century Street 13 D2
New Chapel Street 8 G2
New Church Street 18 H3
New House (Gilfach Goch) 15 A4
New Houses (Clydach Vale)
 ....12 G2
New Houses (M. Tydfil) 20 F2
New King Street..................9 A6
New Mill Corner.................17 D2
New Mill Gardens 17 D1
New Park Crescent 32 G4
New Park Terrace 32 G4
New Road (Abercynon) 26 E1
New Road (Aberdare) 2 F4
New Road (M. Tydfil)..........20 E4
New Road (Mt. Ash)
 ....6 H2/23 A2/C3
New Road (Penrhiwceiber) 24 E6
New Road (Ynysybwl)........29 C2
New Row 43 B6
New Scales Houses 2 H3
New Street (Abercynon) 26 G5
New Street (Aberdare) 5 D1
New Street (Caerphilly) 41 D1
New Street (Ferndale) 10 F5
New Street (Treherbert).......7 A3
New Tynybedw Street 8 G3
New Villas 5 C4
Newbridge Court 32 F1
Newbridge Road 35 D3
Newcastle Street 21 A1
Newfound Terrace 19 C6
Newmarket Walk 21 A1
Newport Road (Bedwas)
 ....42 G2/43 A2
Newport Road (Machen) 43 A5
Newton Street 21 C6
Newton Villas*, John St. ...23 D4
Newydd Court 37 C3
Neyland Close 34 H3
Niagara Street 32 F3
Nibloe Terrace 19 D4
Nicholas Close 37 C6
Nicholas Court....................8 H6
Nightingale Gardens 34 F4
Nightingale Street 21 C6
Nightingales Bush 32 G2
Nile Road (Pontypridd) 32 F3
Nile Road (Tonypandy) 13 D1
Ninian Street (Treherbert) ...7 C5
Ninian Street (Treorchy) 8 F2
Ninth Avenue....................19 D3
Nith Street 3 C4
Nixonville.........................24 G1
Noel Terrace 24 G1
Norfolk Court 37 A5
Norman Terrace (M. Tydfil) 19 B6
Norman Terrace*, Dyffryn Road
 ....21 D6
North Avenue 3 B3
North Road (Ferndale).......10 E3
North Road (Porth) 14 H3
North Street (Abercynon) ..26 G5
North Street (Dowlais) 20 E4
North Street (M. Tydfil) 20 E4

North Street (Pontypridd)....**32** F1
North Terrace (Blaen Clydach)
....................................**12** H2
North Terrace (Maerdy).........**9** A1
North View (Taff's Well).....**38** H5
North View Terrace (Aberaman)
...................................**5** D2
North View Terrace (Caerphilly)
...................................**42** E5
Nuns Crescent....................**31** D1
Nursery Rise **42** F1
Nythbran Terrace...............**29** A4

O
Oak Close **35** C5
Oak Court **37** C2
Oak Hill Villas **3** B3
Oak House **37** D5
Oak Lane............................**43** D6
Oak Road (Llanharry) **15** A6
Oak Road (M. Tydfil) **19** B4
Oak Street (Aberdare).........**3** C4
Oak Street (Clydach Vale) **12** G2
Oak Street (Ferndale) **10** F4
Oak Street (Gelli)................**9** A6
Oak Street (Gilfach Goch)..**15** A5
Oak Street (Rhydyfelin)......**39** A1
Oak Street (Treherbert).......**7** D6
Oak Street (Treorchy)..........**8** G3
Oak Street Close.................**39** A1
Oak Terrace (Abercwmboi) ..**6** F2
Oak Terrace (Mt. Ash).......**23** D6
Oak Tree Court **8** F2
Oakbrook Drive **1** C2
Oakdale Road **13** C5
Oakdale Terrace **13** C5
Oakfield Crescent **39** A6
Oakfield Gardens **43** D5
Oakfield Street **22** G5
Oakfield Terrace **11** B4
Oakland Close.....................**1** C2
Oakland Street (Bedlinog)..**28** H6
Oakland Street (Mt. Ash)...**23** C5
Oakland Terrace **10** G5
Oakland Villas....................**10** G6
Oaklands (Merthyr Vale)...**24** H3
Oaklands (Miskin)..............**17** D1
Oaklands (Trehafod).........**29** C5
Oaklands (Troedyrhiw)......**22** G3
Oaklands Crescent **30** H5
Oaklands Drive...................**9** B5
Oaklands Terrace (Cilfynydd)
.................................**30** H5
Oaklands Terrace (Treharris)
...................................**27** B2
Oakley Terrace **13** C5
Oaks, The (Aberdare) **3** A3
Oaks, The (Church Village)
..........................**33** B1/**34** F5
Oaks, The (Machen)...........**43** D6
Oaks, The (Quaker's Yard) **27** C4
Oakwood Court **3** A3
Oakwood Drive **16** F5
Oakwood Street **32** G6
Ocean Street **8** F6
Odessa Street **20** E3
Odet Court...........................**37** D4
Office Houses **3** D2
Office Row **11** B6
Office Street **14** H4
Ogmore Court **41** A3
Olcote House......................**34** H3
Old Brithweunydd Road ...**13** C2

Old Caerphilly Road*, Tyla Gwyn
...................................**38** F2
Old Cemetery Road............**26** F4
Old Chapel Road................**18** G4
Old Church Street **18** H4
Old Danyderi **24** G1
Old Farm Lane*, Ffordd Dinefwr
...................................**36** H6
Old Field Road **37** D3
Old Garden Court **37** B5
Old Mill Lane*, High St......**19** C6
Old Nantgarw Road **38** G1/**41** A6
Old Parish Road **29** D2
Old Park Terrace...............**32** G4
Old Penrhys Road......**9** D6/**11** A2
Old School Close **18** G2/**19** A6
Old School Court **37** B2
Old Station Yard (Caerphilly)
...................................**42** G1
Old Station Yard (Treharris)
...................................**27** A3
Old Street **11** A6
Old Winch Fawr Road **18** F6
Old Ynysybwl Road **25** B5
Olive Terrace **14** F5
Oliver Street **31** C2
Oliver Terrace **32** G5
Orchard Close (Aberfan)....**22** G6
Orchard Close (Porth) **29** A4
Orchard Drive **30** E4
Orchard Grove....................**37** A4
Osband Flats **41** C3
Osbourne Terrace **23** D6
Other Street........................**25** C5
Oval, The **21** B1
Overton Street **20** E3
Owen Street **32** H6
Oxford Buildings*, Oxford Street
...................................**23** C3
Oxford Street (Aberdare)....**3** B3
Oxford Street (Maerdy) **9** B2
Oxford Street (Mt. Ash)....**23** B3
Oxford Street (Nantgarw) ..**38** E1
Oxford Street (Treforest) ...**32** G5

P
Packers Road **14** G2
Paddocks Crescent **17** A3
Paddocks, The (Aberdare) ..**4** E5
Paddocks, The (Church Village)
...................................**34** F3
Paddocks, The (Tonyrefail) **16** H2
Paget Street **25** C6
Painters Row **7** D6
Palalwyf Avenue **17** B2
Palm Road..........................**19** B3
Palmers Row **14** G5
Pamela Street **23** B3
Pandy Close **19** A5
Pandy Cottages.................**27** C3
Pandy Lane.........................**43** C5
Pandy Road........................**42** E1
Pandy View **27** D3
Pandy, The **1** B2
Pant Close **20** E1
Pant Cottages **20** E1
Pant Du Road **30** H3
Pant Garw Villas*,
   Llantrisant Road..........**33** B1
Pant Llygodfa....................**41** B6
Pant Mawr Road **42** E1
Pant Place **38** F4
Pant Road..................**20** E1/E2/F2

Pant Terrace **20** E3
Pant y Cerdin......................**4** F5
Pant y Dderwen.................**35** A6
Pant y Fedwen **5** D1
Pant y Seren **16** F6
Pant yr Eos **4** E1
Pantanas Cottages **27** A3
Pantanas Estate **27** B3
Panteg Cottages **25** C6
Pantglas Close **43** A2
Pantglas Fawr **22** G5
Pantglas Road....................**22** G6
Pantglas View **43** A2
Pantgwynlais **37** C3
Pantycelyn Drive **41** D2
Pantycelynen **18** F2
Pantyffyn Road **19** D5/**21** C1
Pantygraigwen Road..........**31** C1
Pantyscallog Terrace........**20** F1
Parade, The (Church Village)
...................................**34** G4
Parade, The (Ferndale).....**10** E3
Parade, The (M. Tydfil) **21** B1
Parade, The (Pentre).........**8** H5
Parade, The (Pontypridd) ..**32** F1
Parade, The (Porth)...........**14** H3
Parc Afon **14** E2
Parc Avenue **42** F2
Parc Cae Felin.....................**1** C2
Parc Castell y Mynach.......**36** H5
Parc Cottages **40** E2
Parc Glas **2** F6
Parc Nant Celyn **34** G1/H6
Parc Newydd **35** C5
Parc Ponty Pandy **42** F2
Parc Terrace (Senghenydd)
...................................**40** E2
Parc Wenallt **27** B2
Parc y Bryn (Creigiau)....**36** H5
Parc y Bryn (Llan. Fardre)
...........................**33** B1/**34** F5
Parc y Coed **36** H6
Parc y Felin (Caerphilly) ...**42** E4
Parc y Felin (Creigiau).......**36** H6
Parc y Fro **36** H5
Parc y Nant.........................**38** G2
Parfitt Close **11** D1
Parfitt Terrace **21** B1
Parish Road........................**34** D6
Park Avenue **42** H1
Park Close (Treforest) **32** F5
Park Close (Treherbert)......**7** C5
Park Cottages **8** E4
Park Crescent (M. Tydfil)...**21** B1
Park Crescent (Pontyclun)..**17** A2
Park Crescent (Porth) **14** G3
Park Crescent (Treharris) ..**27** A2
Park Crescent (Treorchy) ...**8** F4
Park Grove **3** B2
Park Hill (Mt. Ash) **23** B3
Park Hill (Penrhiwceiber)...**23** D5
Park Lane (Aberdare) ..**2** G6/**3** A2
Park Lane (Caerphilly).......**41** D5
Park Lane (Groes-faen).....**36** F6
Park Lane (Taff's Well) **38** F5
Park Lane (Tonyrefail).......**16** H2
Park Lane (Treharris) **27** A3
Park Place (Cilfynydd).......**30** H3
Park Place (Maerdy) **9** A1
Park Place (M. Tydfil) **19** C6
Park Place (Tonypandy) ...**13** A1
Park Place (Treherbert) **7** B4
Park Place (Troedyrhiw) ...**22** G4

Park Prospect **32** E1
Park Road (Aberdare) **4** E5
Park Road (Cwmparc) **8** E4/E6
Park Road (Ferndale) **10** F5
Park Road (Maerdy)............**9** A1
Park Road (Radyr)..............**37** A5
Park Road (Tonypandy) **13** C3
Park Row (8) **19** B5
Park Row Gardens **19** B5
Park Side Lane **32** E2
Park Street (Abercynon) ...**26** F6
Park Street (Clydach Vale) **12** F2
Park Street (Mt. Ash)........**23** D5
Park Street (Porth) **14** G2
Park Street (Treforest) **32** G4
Park Street (Tylorstown) ...**10** G6
Park Terrace (Cwmparc) **8** E4/E6
Park Terrace (Llanharan) ..**17** D5
Park Terrace (M. Tydfil)....**19** C6
Park Terrace (Pentrebach) **21** D6
Park Terrace (Trelewis).....**27** C3
Park View (Abercynon) **26** G3/G4
Park View (Cwmaman) **5** B4
Park View (Gelli) **9** A6
Park View (Llanharan).......**17** D6
Park View (Llantrisant) **35** C4
Park View (Merthyr Vale) ..**24** G2
Park View (Tylorstown) **12** E1
Park View (Ynyshir)..........**12** D1
Park View Terrace (Abercwmboi)
...................................**6** F2
Park View Terrace (Aberdare)
...................................**3** D2
Park View Terrace (M. Tydfil)
...................................**18** E2
Park Villas **3** B2
Park Way*, Park Terrace....**19** C6
Park, The **27** A2
Parkdale View **35** D4
Parkfield Road **4** F4
Parklands Crescent...........**16** G3
Parklands Road..................**16** G3
Parrish Place **40** F2
Parry Street (Pentre)....**8** H6/**9** A5
Parry Street (Tylorstown) ..**11** D2
Parrys Drive **26** E3
Partridge Avenue **11** B4
Partridge Road **11** B3
Partridge Square **11** C4
Partridge Street **9** A5
Pasteur Grove **34** F4
Patch, The **15** B6
Patmore Close **38** F6
Pearces Court **18** G3
Pearse Lane **21** B3
Pearson Crescent **30** F4
Pembroke Close (Church Village)
...................................**34** H3
Pembroke Close (M. Tydfil) **18** F5
Pembroke Close (Ystrad)
...........................**9** C6/**11** A2
Pembroke Court **41** A4
Pembroke Crescent...........**35** A1
Pembroke Place **19** D5
Pembroke Street (Aberdare) **3** C3
Pembroke Street (Tonyrefail)
...................................**16** F6
Pembroke Street (Troedyrhiw)
...................................**22** G2
Pen Bryn Hendy **17** C1
Pen Darren **14** F5
Pen Dinas **13** D2
Pen Dinas Flats..................**13** D2

Pen Gurnos 19 A3
Pen Hendy.......................17 C1
Pen Llew Court 2 G6/3 A2
Pen Pych Close 7 A3
Pen Rhiw Road 9 A6
Pen Twyn Road..................8 G4
Pen Tyntyla 11 C2
Pen y Banc 14 F5
Pen y Bryn (Penywaun).......2 E4
Pen y Cae 42 G3
Pen y Darren Close 32 E1
Pen y Darren Drive 37 D6
Pen y Dre (Caerphilly) 41 B1
Pen y Dre (Porth)............14 F6
Pen y Ffordd 41 C3
Pen y Fro 2 F6
Pen y Groes (Caerphilly) ...41 B1
Pen y Groes (Groes-faen) ..36 F6
Pen y Groes (Treharris).....27 C1
Pen y Mynydd 30 F3
Pen y Parc.....................33 C6
Pen y Rhiw 9 D6/11 A2
Pen yr Allt 41 C6
Pen yr Eglwys 33 B1/34 F5
Pen yr Heol 2 E3
Penbury Court 37 A4
Pencai Terrace..................8 F3
Pencerrig Street...............32 E2
Penclawdd......................42 G2
Pencoed Avenue.............32 G2
Pencoed Cottages..............2 G2
Pendarren Gardens.........19 C5
Pendarren Park 19 C6
Pendarren Road 19 C6
Pendarren Street 3 B3
Penderyn Place 3 D5
Pendre Crescent 17 D4
Pendwyallt 37 D4
Pendyrus Court 12 E1
Pengarddu 20 H2
Penheol Ely Road 32 G1
Penheolferthyr 21 C1
Penlan View 18 G2
Penllwyn Lane 43 A5/D1
Penllwyn Terrace.............12 E3
Penlocks 27 A4
Penmaesglas Terrace 13 B2
Penmain Street 14 G2
Penmark Row 1 A1
Penn Street 27 B2
Penparlas......................14 F3
Penpisgah Road 13 B3
Penquesta Cottages 17 C3
Penrhiw Fer Road (Tonypandy)
........................13 C5
Penrhiw Fer Road (Tonyrefail)
........................16 E1
Penrhiw Lane 43 C4
Penrhiw Road 31 D4
Penrhiwceiber Road 23 C4
Penrhiwgwynt Road 14 H3
Penrhos (Llan. Fardre)
........................33 B1/34 F6
Penrhos (Radyr) 37 A4
Penrhys Avenue 11 D3
Penrhys Road (Tylorstown)11 D3
Penrhys Road (Ystrad)
........................9 D6/11 B2
Penrhys Uchaf................11 D3
Penry Street....................21 A1
Pentre Court 9 A5
Pentre House.....................9 A4
Pentre Road (Maerdy)..........9 A2

Pentre Road (Pentre) ..8 H4/9 A4
Pentrebach Road (M. Tydfil)
........................21 B3
Pentrebach Road (Pontypridd)
........................32 G3
Pentrebane Street 41 D5
Pentwyn (Caerphilly) 41 B2
Pentwyn (Radyr) 37 A5
Pentwyn (Tonyrefail) 16 E5
Pentwyn Avenue 25 C1
Pentwyn Cottages 17 D4
Pentwyn Court...................1 D3
Pentwyn Deintyr 27 A5
Pentwyn Isaf 41 C1
Pentwyn Isaf Rise 41 C1
Pentwyn Road 27 B4
Pentwyn Villas 19 B5
Penuel Lane 32 E2
Penuel Street..................21 B1
Penyard Road (Hirwaun).....1 B1
Penyard Road (M. Tydfil) ..19 C6
Penybryn (Pontypridd).......30 F4
Penybryn Estate 19 D4
Penybryn Garden City 19 D4
Penybryn Road 23 D6
Penybryn Street (Aberdare)..3 B2
Penybryn Street (Gilfach Goch)
........................15 B5
Penybryn Terrace 23 D6
Penybryn View................20 E6
Penybryn Villas 19 D5
Penycoed Cae Caravan Park
........................33 C5
Penycoedcae Road..........33 C6
Penydarren Gardens........19 C5
Penydarren Park 19 C5/C6
Penydre (M. Tydfil) 19 A3
Penyfan View..................19 B3
Penygarreg Road 16 G6
Penygraig Road 13 C3
Penygraig Terrace 25 C6
Penylan Road 31 D3
Penylan Street.................21 D6
Penywaun 34 F2
Penywrlod 28 H2
Pergwm Street 14 E1
Perrott Place 27 B3
Perrott Street 27 B3
Perthigleision Bridge*, Bryntaf
........................24 G1
Perthlwyd.........................1 D3
Perthygleision Crescent ...24 G2
Phillip Row 4 G5
Phillip Street (Aberdare) 3 C2
Phillip Street (Mt. Ash)......23 C2
Phillip Street (Pontypridd) ..32 E4
Phillips Terrace (M. Tydfil)..21 B2
Phillips Terrace (Senghenydd)
........................40 E1
Phillips Terrace (Trehafod) 29 B5
Phyllis Street 22 G2
Picadilly Square..................42 E4
Picton Terrace 17 D5
Pine Close 19 B3
Pine Court (Llan. Fardre)...36 H1
Pine Court (Talbot Grn.) 35 A4
Pine Court (Tongwynlais) ..37 C2
Pine Street.....................10 F4
Pine Tree Way 28 E6
Pinecroft Avenue 4 F4
Pines, The (Hirwaun)..........1 C2
Pines, The (Trethomas)....43 D3
Pinewalk Drive................29 A5

Pinewood Avenue 39 B2
Pinewood Drive 13 C1
Pinewood Hill...................35 A4
Pinewood View 30 E4
Pit Place 4 G4
Pit Row 5 C3
Plane Grove 19 C3
Plane Street....................39 A2
Plantation Close 19 D5
Plantation Gardens...........26 G4
Plantation Road 26 F5
Plantation Square 22 F2
Plantation Terrace............22 G5
Plas Carmel*, Graigwen Road
........................32 E2
Plas Cwm Parc 40 E2
Plas Derwen 22 F1
Plas Grug 41 C6
Plas Horeb........................7 B5
Plas Nant 40 F5
Plas Phillips 41 C4
Plas Thomas 41 D5
Plas y Fedwen 30 F3
Plasdraw Avenue 3 D3
Plasdraw Court*, Plasdraw Road
........................3 D3
Plasdraw Place 3 D3
Plasdraw Road 3 D3
Plasmarl 2 G3
Plasydarren*, Heol Gerrig ..18 E2
Pleasant Grove 4 G4
Pleasant Heights.............14 G2
Pleasant Hill....................10 F4
Pleasant Place 41 B2
Pleasant Road 13 C3
Pleasant Street..................8 H4
Pleasant Terrace (Clydach Vale)
........................12 G2
Pleasant Terrace (Ystrad) ...9 C6
Pleasant View (Aberdare) ...5 D1
Pleasant View (Aberfan) ...22 G4
Pleasant View (Beddau) ...33 C6
Pleasant View (Bedlinog) ..28 H5
Pleasant View (M. Tydfil) ..18 G3
Pleasant View (Mynachdy) 25 A3
Pleasant View (Pentre) 9 A5
Pleasant View (Pontypridd) 32 F1
Pleasant View (Tonypandy)
........................13 C6
Pleasant View (Tonyrefail)..16 F3
Pleasant View (Trehafod) ..28 B6
Pleasant View (Treharris) ..27 A3
Pleasant View (Troedyrhiw)
........................22 G3
Pleasant View (Tylorstown)12 E2
Pleasant View (Wattstown) 12 F4
Pleasant View (Ynysybwl) ..25 C6
Pleasant View Street (9) ...19 B5
Plymouth Houses 21 B3
Plymouth Road (Pontypridd)
........................31 C1
Plymouth Road (Radyr)......37 B6
Plymouth Street...............21 B2
Plymouth Terrace*, Plymouth St.
........................21 B3
Poets Close 39 A1
Poets End 17 C6
Police Houses (Aberdare) ...2 H3
Police Houses (Aberfan) ...22 G5
Police Houses (Bedlinog) ..28 G5
Police Houses (Gilfach Goch)
........................15 B5
Police Houses (Llantrisant) 35 C3

Police Houses (Tonyrefail) 16 G6
Police Houses*, Brynifor 23 C4
Pond Place 4 G4
Ponds Row 21 B5
Pont Pendre Caravan Park 39 C4
Pont y Capel Road 18 G4
Pontmorlais West 19 C6
Pontmorlais*, High Street ..19 C6
Pontpren.........................1 B6
Pontrhondda Avenue 9 D6/11 B3
Pontrhondda Road 11 B3
Pontsarn Close 19 B1
Pontsarn Road.................19 B1
Pontshonnorton Road 30 G6
Pontycynon Terrace..........26 F3
Pontygwaith 24 H6
Pontygwindy Road 41 D1
Pontypandy Lane..............42 E3
Pontypridd Road 14 H3
Poplar House...................37 D5
Poplar Mews 22 G3
Poplar Place (M. Tydfil) 18 H1
Poplar Place (Troedyrhiw)..22 G3
Poplar Road (Caerphilly) ...42 F5
Poplar Road (Rhydyfelin) ..39 A2
Poplar Street 22 G3
Poplar Terrace.................21 D6
Poplar Way 19 B3
Poplars, The (Llanharry) ...15 B6
Poplars, The (Mt. Ash) 23 C3
Poplars, The (Rhydyfelin) ..39 C4
Porcher Avenue 30 F4
Porset Close 42 F5
Porset Drive 42 E5
Porset Park 42 F4
Porset Row 42 G2
Porth Place 14 H3
Porth Relief Road 12 E3/14 G3
Porth Street....................14 H3
Portreeve Close...............35 D4
Post Office Lane (M. Tydfil) 21 A1
Post Office Lane (Treharris)
........................27 A4
Post Office Row 38 E4
Post Office Row*, De Winton St.
........................11 B6
Potters Field 2 G5
Powell Drive....................17 B6
Powell Street...................28 G6
Powells Place 14 H3
Powys Place 32 H5
Powys Road 39 D6
Precinct, The 39 A6
Presteigne Avenue 34 H3
Pretoria Road 16 H3
Price Street (M. Tydfil).......18 H3
Price Street (Pentre) 8 H3
Price Street*, Ynys Llwyd Street
........................3 C4
Primrose Close (Nelson) ...27 D5
Primrose Close (Pant) 20 E2
Primrose Cottages
(Gwaelod-y-garth) 38 E4
Primrose Cottages (Hirwaun)
........................1 B1
Primrose Cottages*, Union Street
........................21 B1
Primrose Court 16 H2
Primrose Hill (Aberdare)
........................2 H5/3 D1
Primrose Hill (M. Tydfil) 21 B2
Primrose Hill (Pentre) 9 B5
Primrose House...............35 A6

Primrose Lane.....

Primrose Lane 27 D5
Primrose Street 13 A1
Primrose Terrace (Aberdare)
.....................................4 E5
Primrose Terrace (Porth) ...29 A4
Primrose Villas*, Llwycoed Road
.....................................2 H4
Princes Avenue 42 E6
Princes Rise 42 E6
Princes Street (Treherbert) ..7 D6
Princes Terrace (Treorchy) ..8 G3
Princess Louise Road 11 B4
Princess Street (Blaenllechau)
...................................10 F3
Princess Street (Gelli) 9 B6
Princess Street (Treforest) 32 G4
Priory Close 32 E1
Priscilla Terrace.................27 C1
Pritchard Street (Tonyrefail)
...................................16 G3
Pritchard Street (Treharris) 27 B2
Prospect Place (Bedlinog)..28 H5
Prospect Place (Cwmaman) 5 B3
Prospect Place (Treorchy) ..8 G2
Prospect Place (Tylorstown)
..........................10 H6/12 E1
Prospect Place*, Pendarren Rd.
...................................19 C6
Prosser Street (Mt. Ash) ...23 D5
Prosser Street (Treharris) ..27 A3
Protheroe Street 10 F5
Pryce Street (Mt. Ash) 23 B3
Pryce Street (Pentre)...........9 A5
Pwllfa Place 5 A4
Pwllfa Road 5 C3
Pwllgwaun Cottages 31 C2
Pwllgwaun Road 31 D2
Pwllhelyg 37 C3
Pwllypant Roundabout 41 D1
Pytchley Close 36 E5

Q

Quakers View 26 H2
Quarry Cottages 23 B3
Quarry Hill Close 31 D2
Quarry Road (Mt. Ash) 23 B3
Quarry Road (Pontypridd)..31 D2
Quarry Row 19 B6
Quarry Street (Ferndale) ...10 G6
Quarry Street (Nantgarw) ..38 F1
Quay Row 21 B4
Queen Charlotte Drive*,
   Cardiff Road...............36 H6
Queen Street (Aberdare).....4 E6
Queen Street (Cwmdare) ...2 F6
Queen Street (M. Tydfil) ...20 F2
Queen Street (Pentre).........8 H4
Queen Street (Ton Pentre)
.............................8 H5/9 A5
Queen Street (Tongwynlais)
...................................37 B2
Queen Street (Treforest)....32 G4
Queens Drive 33 B2/34 F6
Queens Road 19 D6/21 B1
Queens Square 12 E2
Queens Terrace.................22 F3
Queensway 38 G2

R

Rachel Street 3 C4
Radnor Drive 34 H3
Radnor Way 14 G6
Raglan Court 41 B3

Raglan Grove....................18 F5
Railway Cottages (Caerphilly)
...................................41 C5
Railway Cottages (Llan. Fardre)
..........................33 B1/34 F6
Railway Side 14 F2
Railway Street (Aberdare) 3 B2
Railway Street (Trelewis) ...27 C2
Railway Terrace (Blaen Clydach)
...................................12 H2
Railway Terrace (Caerphilly)
...................................42 E6
Railway Terrace (Cwmparc) 8 F6
Railway Terrace (Hirwaun) ..1 B1
Railway Terrace (Llan. Fardre)
..........................33 B1/34 F6
Railway Terrace (M. Tydfil) 21 B3
Railway Terrace (Mt. Ash) ..24 E6
Railway Terrace (Talbot Grn.)
...................................35 B5
Railway Terrace (Tongwynlais)
...................................37 B3
Railway Terrace (Tonypandy)
...................................13 B2
Railway Terrace (Treharris) 27 B2
Railway Terrace (Ynysbir) ..12 G6
Railway View (Llwynypia) ..11 B4
Railway View (Williamstown)
...................................13 C4
Ralph Street......................32 F1
Ramah Street......................8 F2
Rambler Court 4 H6
Raven Court*, Hillside Ter. ..9 B6
Ravenhill Street 9 B6
Ravensbrook 37 A3
Raymond Terrace 32 G5
Rear Dunraven Street*,
   Dunraven Street..........13 B1
Rectory Close (Caerphilly) 41 D6
Rectory Close (M. Tydfil) ...20 F3
Rectory Gardens (Bedwas) 42 H1
Rectory Gardens (Machen) 43 C5
Rectory Road (Bedwas) 42 H1
Rectory Road (Caerphilly) ..41 D6
Rectory Road (Gelligaer)....28 H2
Red Dragon Cottages*,
   Heol Sticil y Beddau.....35 C4
Red Roofs Close 17 A6
Red Rose Hill.....................9 B5
Redbrook Avenue 43 B2
Redbrook Close.................41 D6
Redbrook Lane 43 C2
Redfield Street 9 C6/11 A2
Redhill Close 1 A2
Redwood Drive (Aberdare) ..2 F6
Redwood Drive (Llan. Fardre)
...................................36 H1
Rees Place 8 H4
Rees Row 20 H3
Rees Street (Dowlais) 20 F2
Rees Street (Gelli) 9 A6
Rees Street (M. Tydfil).......21 B2
Rees Street (Treorchy) 8 G3
Rees Terrace 32 G5
Regent Close 4 E6
Regent Street (Dowlais) 20 E3
Regent Street (Ferndale) ...10 F5
Regent Street (Treorchy) 8 G3
Regents Street (Aberdare) ..4 E6
Reigate Terrace 36 F6
Rheidol Close (Cwmbach) ...4 F4
Rheidol Close (Treorchy) 7 D6
Rheola Street....................24 E6

Rheolau Terrace 29 B5
Rhigos Road (Hirwaun) 1 A2
Rhigos Road (Treorchy)..7 A1/B4
Rhiw Ceris 4 F4
Rhiw Fach 41 B2
Rhiw Felin 39 A1
Rhiw Nant 4 E2
Rhiw'r Ddar 38 F4/G4
Rhiw'r Ddar House.............38 F5
Rhiwfer 27 D6
Rhiwgarn Road 14 F6
Rhiwsaeson Road 36 E5
Rhodfa Newydd 4 F5
Rhodfa Road 20 E1
Rhodfa Terrace 22 G2
Rhondda Fechan Farm Estate
...................................10 E4
Rhondda Road (Ferndale)..10 E3
Rhondda Road (Pontypridd)
.........................31 D2/32 E2
Rhondda Terrace (Ferndale)
...................................10 F5
Rhondda Terrace (Llwynypia)
...................................11 B4
Rhos Bedw 14 G5
Rhos Helyg 42 G3
Rhos Nathan Wyn 3 D5
Rhos Street 41 D3
Rhosdyfed 3 D5
Rhoshyfryd 1 A4
Rhossili Close 1 A2
Rhuddlan Court 41 A3
Rhyd y Gwern Close 42 G2
Rhyd y Gwern Isaf 43 C5
Rhyd y Gwern Lane...........43 C6
Rhyd y Nant 17 B2
Rhyd yr Heleg 38 E1
Rhydfach 21 D6
Rhymney Cottages 38 G5
Rhymney Terrace 41 D5
Rhys Street (Tonypandy)
.........................11 B6/13 B1
Rhys Street (Tylorstown)....12 E4
Rhys Street (Williamstown) 13 D5
Richard Street (Abercwmboi)6 F2
Richard Street (Cilfynydd) ..30 H4
Richard Street (Maerdy) 9 B2
Richards Terrace (Cwmbach)
.....................................4 G6
Richards Terrace (Tonypandy)
...................................11 B6
Richards Terrace (Trelewis)
...................................27 C2
Richmond Drive 1 A1
Richmond Road 23 B2
Richmond Terrace 4 E2
Rickard Terrace 32 E3
Rickards Street (Pontypridd)
...................................32 E3
Rickards Street (Porth) 14 H4
Ridgeway 43 C2
Ridgeway Close 31 D1
Ridgeway Place 39 A6
Ridings, The (Aberdare) 3 A3
Ridings, The (Tonteg) 39 A6
Rink, The 19 C6
Rise, The (Aberdare) 2 A3
Rise, The (Church Village) 34 H3
Rise, The (Gelli) 9 B6
Rise, The (M. Tydfil) 20 F1
Rise, The (Rhydyfelin).......39 C4
Rise, The (Ynyshir) 14 G1
River Glade 38 F6

River Row (Abercanaid) 21 C6
River Row (Pontyclun)......17 A1
River Row (Treherbert) 7 C6
River Row*, Ynysmeurig Road
...................................26 G5
River Street (Treforest) 32 G4
River Street (Ystrad) 9 C6
River Terrace (Porth) 14 H4
River Terrace (Treorchy) 8 F7
River View (Tonypandy) 13 B1
River Walk 21 A1
Rivers Edge 17 B2
Riverside 1 C2
Riverside Close (Merthyr Vale)
...................................24 G1
Riverside Close*, Avon Terrace
...................................12 H6
Riverside Court 40 E3
Riverside Park 19 B5
Riverside Street 38 F4
Riverside Terrace 43 B5
Riverside Villas 14 F2
Roam Road 35 D3
Roam Road Terrace 35 D3
Robert Street (Llanharan) ..17 D5
Robert Street (Pentre)........8 H4
Robert Street (Ynysybwl) ..29 C1
Roberts Avenue 19 D3
Roberts Lane 21 B1
Rock Cottages 31 D1
Rock Drive 9 A6
Rock Houses 27 A4
Rock Lane 18 H4
Rock Street 25 A5
Rock Terrace 25 A5
Rock View 26 H1
Rock Villas 26 H1
Rockingstone Terrace 32 G2
Rockwood Road 38 G5
Rocky Road 19 D3
Rodericks Terrace 27 A4
Rogart Terrace 30 F5
Roman Ridge 28 H2
Rookwood Close 19 B5
Rose Cottages (Machen) ...43 C5
Rose Cottages (Nelson) 27 D6
Rose Cottages (Treharris) ..27 B5
Rose Cottages*, Glancynon St.
...................................23 C3
Rose Cottages*, Main Rd...38 B4
Rose Hill 27 A4
Rose Row 4 H6
Rose Terrace 17 C6
Rosedale Terrace 11 B5
Rosehill Terrace 15 B1
Ross Close 31 D5
Ross Rise 7 C5
Rosser Street (Ferndale) ...10 F5
Rosser Street (Pontypridd) 31 D3
Roundabout Court 42 E1
Rowan Close (Mt. Ash) 23 C3
Rowan Close (Nelson) 27 D5
Rowan Close (Pontypridd) 31 D5
Rowan Court (Aberdare) 3 A3
Rowan Court (Llanharry) ...15 A6
Rowan Gardens 34 G5
Rowan Rise 18 H2
Rowan Tree Lane 17 D1
Rowan Way 19 B4
Rowley Terrace 9 B2
Rowling Street 13 C4
Royal Cottages 9 B2
Royal Crescent 19 D5

.....**Station Terrace (Cwmaman)**

Royal Oak 43 D6
Royal Oak Close 43 D5
Royal Terrace 13 C1
Rudry Close 42 G2
Rudry Road.......................42 G2
Ruperra Court 32 F1
Ruperra Street...................35 D3
Russell Street 20 E4
Russell Terrace*, Hampton St.
....21 B2
Russell Villas.....................22 G5
Ruthin Way 34 H3

S

Salem Baptist Flats*, Talbot Rd.
....35 C4
Salem Lane 34 H4
Salem Terrace
   (Gwaelod-y-garth) 38 E4
Salem Terrace (Tonypandy)
....11 B4
Salisbury Close 18 E1
Salisbury Road 26 F5
Salop Street......................42 E5
Sand Street (6) 19 B6
Sandbrook Villas*, Union Street
....21 B1
Sandy Bank Road 9 C5
Sarah Street 24 H1
Sardis Road.......................31 D3
Saron Street 32 G4
Saxon Street 19 B6
Scales Row 4 F5
Scarborough Road 32 G1
School Close 27 D6
School Lane (Gwaelod-y-garth)
....38 F5
School Lane (Rhydyfelin) ...39 A3
School Road (Pontyclun)....17 D2
School Road (Troedyrhiw) 22 G2
School Street (Abercwmboi) 6 F2
School Street (Blaencwm)....7 A6
School Street (Cymmer) 14 H4
School Street (Ferndale) 10 F3
School Street (Llantrisant)..35 C3
School Street (Maerdy) 9 A2
School Street (Pontyclun) ...17 B1
School Street (Porth)..........14 H2
School Street (Senghenydd)
....40 F2
School Street (Ton Pentre) ..9 A6
School Street (Tonypandy) 13 D4
School Street (Tonyrefail) ..16 G3
School Street (Tylorstown) 12 E3
School Street (Wattstown)..12 F4
School Terrace (Llanharan)17 D6
School Terrace (Tonypandy)
....11 A6
School View.......................28 E5
Scott Street 7 B4
Seaton Place 31 D2
Seaton Street 31 D2
Second Avenue (Caerphilly)
....41 C3
Second Avenue (M. Tydfil) 19 C3
Sefton Court 37 A5
Selina Road.......................26 E2
Senghenydd Street 8 F3
Seventh Avenue 19 C3
Severn Road 39 C5
Seward Street 19 D5
Seymour Avenue...............17 D4
Seymour Street (Aberdare) ..3 C3

Seymour Street (Mt. Ash) ..23 C2
Shadow Wood Drive 17 C1
Shady Road.........................9 B6
Shakespeare Rise 39 A1
Shelley Court....................43 D1
Shelley Walk 39 A1
Sheppard Street 31 D2
Sherwood Street 11 B4
Shingrig Road 27 D4
Shire Court 27 C3
Shirley Drive 18 E1
Shirley Gardens................18 E1
Shop Houses......................2 H4
Shrewsbury Avenue...........14 F6
Sierra Pines 6 H4
Siloam Hill 43 B5
Siloh Lane*, Newcastle St. 21 A1
Silverhill Close..................30 H5
Silverton Drive 36 E5
Simon Terrace...................13 D4
Sion Place 4 G5
Sion Street........................32 F2
Sion Terrace 4 G5
Siop y Coed 39 A5
Sir Alfred Owen Way 41 D1
Sir Stafford Close..............42 F2
Six Bells 18 F1
Six Bells Estate 18 F2/H6
Sixth Avenue 19 C3
Slope, The 14 H3
Smith Row 13 D6
Smith Street........................9 A6
Smiths Court 20 H3
Snowden Court 42 F4
Somerset Close.................18 G3
Somerset Lane 18 G3
Somerset Place*, Union St. 21 B1
South Avenue 3 B3
South Drive 35 D4
South Glade 38 F6
South Pandy Road 42 E3
South Street (Abercynon) ..26 G5
South Street (Dowlais)......20 F4
South Street (Ynyshir).......14 G1
South Terrace 18 H4
South View (Llanharan) 17 B6
South View (Merthyr Vale) 24 H4
South View (Taff's Well) ...38 H5
South View (Troedyrhiw)...22 G2
Southall Street..................17 A5
Southern Street 42 E5
Southgate Avenue.............35 D4
Sovereign Gardens 17 D1
Spencer Lane 39 A3
Spencer Place...................39 A3
Spencer Street....................5 B3
Spring Street 20 E3
Springfield 12 G5
Springfield Close 4 H5
Springfield Cottages ..9 D6/11 A2
Springfield Court 34 G4
Springfield Drive 26 G4
Springfield Gardens...........37 A4
Springfield Road 9 A1
Springfield Terrace (Nelson)
....28 E6
Springfield Terrace (Rhydyfelin)
....32 H5
Spruce Tree Grove 19 B4
Square, The (Abertridwr) ..40 F5
Square, The (Beddau)........33 C6
Square, The (Bedwas) 42 G2
Square, The (Llanharan) ...17 D5

Square, The (Nelson) 28 E5
Square, The (Porth)...........14 H3
Square, The (Tonypandy) ..11 A6
Square, The (Tonyrefail) 16 F6
Square, The (Treharris)......27 B3
Square, The (Troedyrhiw) ..22 G2
Squires Court.....................36 F2
Squires Row 13 D2
St. Aarons Drive 17 C4
St. Albans Cottages.............7 A3
St. Albans Road...................7 A3
St. Albans Terrace...............7 A4
St. Andrews Close....33 B2/34 F6
St. Andrews Court 11 B6
St. Andrews Road 31 D5
St. Annes Drive 33 B2
St. Annes Gardens 40 G5
St. Asaphs Way.................41 D6
St. Athans Court 41 C5
St. Brides Manor 36 H1
St. Catherines Close 42 G1
St. Cattwgs Avenue...........28 H3
St. Cenydd Close...............41 B3
St. Cenydd Road 41 B3/B4
St. Christophers Drive 41 C5
St. Clears Close 41 D5
St. Cynons Court...............11 C4
St. Davids Close (Heolgerrig)
....18 E1
St. Davids Close (Nantgarw)
....38 E1
St. Davids Close (Pentre) 8 H6
St. Davids Close (Porth) 14 G6
St. Davids Cottages*, High Street
....23 B3
St. Davids Drive.................43 C2
St. Davids Heights.............35 C6
St. Davids Place (Llantrisant)
....35 D3
St. Davids Place*, High St. 23 B3
St. Davids Road 17 D2
St. Davids Street 9 A6
St. Davids Way 41 C6
St. Donats Close 18 E6
St. Donats Court 41 C5
St. Fagans Grove 18 E5
St. Fagans Street 41 D5
St. Helens Court 41 D6
St. Ilans Way 41 D6
St. Illtyds Road 34 G3
St. James Close (Caerphilly)
....42 G2
St. James Close (M. Tydfil) 21 D5
St. James Cottages 2 H4
St. James Mews 17 C5
St. Johns Close 18 H3
St. Johns Drive 8 H5
St. Johns Gardens.............21 B2
St. Johns Grove 19 D5
St. Johns Lane 27 C6
St. Johns Road 16 G2
St. Johns Street (Aberdare)
....................................2 H6/3 B1
St. Johns Street (Porth).....14 H4
St. Josephs Terrace 5 B4
St. Julians Court 41 C6
St. Julius Crescent 17 C4
St. Lukes Avenue 39 A3
St. Lukes Close (Dowlais) ..20 E2
St. Lukes Close (Llanharan)
....17 C4
St. Lukes Road 29 A4
St. Margarets Close...........43 A2

St. Margarets Road 41 C5
St. Marks Close 17 C4
St. Martins Crescent 41 D6
St. Martins Road 41 C5
St. Mary Street (Bedwas) ..42 G1
St. Mary Street (Trelewis) ..27 C2
St. Marys Close (M. Tydfil) 19 C5
St. Marys Close (Pontypridd)
....32 G3
St. Marys Close (Treherbert) 7 C5
St. Mellons Court...............41 D5
St. Michaels Avenue 32 F4
St. Michaels Close (Beddau)
....33 C6
St. Michaels Close (Radyr) 37 C2
St. Nicholas Court 41 D5
St. Peters Avenue 17 C6
St. Peters Close (Abercwmboi)
....6 F2
St. Peters Close (Llanharan)
....17 C4
St. Peters Court*, Pentre Road
....8 H4
St. Stephens Avenue..........8 H3
St. Teilos Way 41 C6
St. Tydfils Avenue 21 B1
Stable Yard*, Stables Ct. ...20 F4
Stables Court 20 F4
Stag Street 2 H5/3 B1
Standard Street 43 A2
Standard Terrace 12 G5
Standard View 12 H5
Standard Villas 43 B1
Stanfield Close 21 B5
Stanley Drive 41 D2
Stanley Road 9 A6
Stanley Square 12 E2
Stanley Street 40 E2
Station Approach 17 B1
Station Cottages (Pontyclun)
....17 B1
Station Cottages (Tonypandy)
....13 D2
Station Hill........................24 G1
Station Houses (Creigiau) ..36 H5
Station Houses (M. Tydfil)
....21 B5
Station Place................2 G5/3 A1
Station Road (Abercynon)..26 G5
Station Road (Church Village)
....34 H5
Station Road (Dowlais) 20 F3
Station Road (Hirwaun) 1 A2
Station Road (Maerdy) 9 A1
Station Road (M. Tydfil) 18 G3
Station Road (Pontygwaith)12 E3
Station Road (Radyr)........37 B6
Station Road (Tonypandy) 13 D2
Station Road (Tonyrefail)...16 F3
Station Road (Treorchy) 8 F3
Station Road (Ynyshir) 12 G6
Station Road*,
   Heol Pant y Gored 36 H5
Station Square...................24 H2
Station Street (Aberdare) 3 D3
Station Street (Machen) 43 C5
Station Street (Porth).........14 H3
Station Street (Tonypandy) 13 B2
Station Street (Treherbert) ..7 C5
Station Terrace (Bedlinog) 28 G6
Station Terrace (Caerphilly)
....42 E5
Station Terrace (Cwmaman) 5 C2

Station Terrace (Dowlais) ..**20** G3
Station Terrace (Llan. Fardre)
...............................**33** B1/**34** F6
Station Terrace (Llwynypia)**11** B5
Station Terrace (Merthyr Vale)
...............................**24** H3
Station Terrace (Mt. Ash) ..**23** D5
Station Terrace (Nelson) **28** E5
Station Terrace (Penyrheol)
...............................**41** B3
Station Terrace (Pontyclun)**17** B1
Station Terrace (Senghenydd)
...............................**40** E2
Station Terrace (Treherbert) **7** C5
Station Terrace*, Station Rd.**9** A1
Station View.......................**41** B3
Station Villas **2** G3
Stephens Terrace **26** H4
Stockland Street **41** D5
Stow Hill............................**32** F4
Stradmore Close **38** F4
Strand Street **23** D4
Strand, The **10** F4
Stream Street **23** B3
Stryd y Berllan **15** A6
Stuart Street (Aberdare) **3** C4
Stuart Street (M. Tydfil) **19** B6
Stuart Street (Pontyclun) ...**17** B1
Stuart Street (Treherbert) ...**7** C5
Stuart Street (Treorchy).......**8** F2
Stuart Terrace **35** B4
Summerdale Close **34** H3
Summerfield Drive..............**35** D4
Summerfield Lane **43** C2
Summerfield Place*,
    Gwaunfarren Road......**19** D4
Summerhill..........................**21** B1
Summerhill Place...............**21** B1
Sunningdale........................**41** B5
Sunny Bank (Abertridwr)...**40** H5
Sunny Bank (Blaen Clydach)
...............................**12** H2
Sunny Bank (Porth)...........**14** G1
Sunny Bank (Williamstown)**13** C4
Sunny Bank (Ynyshir) **12** G6
Sunny Bank*, Heol y Beiliau
...............................**35** C4
Sunny Hill **9** A1
Sunnybank (Machen) **43** B5
Sunnybank (Mt. Ash) **24** E6
Sunnybank (Treharris)........**27** B4
Sunnybank Close **19** B6
Sunnybank Street **3** D4
Sunnybank Terrace **8** E4
Sunnyside (Abercynon)......**26** E2
Sunnyside (Pontypridd) **31** D1
Susannah Place **27** A3
Swan Street (Llantrisant)...**35** C3
Swan Street (M. Tydfil) **21** A1
Swan Terrace **13** C3
Swanbridge Court **42** F1
Swansea Road (Hirwaun) **1** B2
Swansea Road (M. Tydfil)
...............................**18** E5/**19** A6
Sweetwater Park **18** H1
Swn y Nant **34** G3
Swn yr Afon (Gilfach Goch) **15** A3
Swn yr Afon (Maerdy) **9** B6
Swn yr Afon (Treorchy) **8** H3
Swyn y Nant **16** E5
Sycamore Close (Aberdare) **3** A2
Sycamore Close (Pontyclun)
...............................**17** D1

Sycamore Crescent...........**18** H1
Sycamore Drive..................**13** C1
Sycamore House................**37** D5
Sycamore Road (Llanharry)
...............................**15** B6
Sycamore Road (M. Tydfil) **19** C4
Sycamore Street (Rhydyfelin)
...............................**39** A2
Sycamore Street (Taff's Well)
...............................**38** F5
Syphon Street **14** H3

T

Tabor Street.......................**38** F5
Taf Olwg **27** C6
Taff Cottages (Llantrisant)..**35** D5
Taff Cottages (Llwynypia) ..**11** B4
Taff Glen View **21** B2
Taff Street (Blaenllechau) ..**10** F3
Taff Street (Gelli) **9** B6
Taff Street (Merthyr Vale) ..**24** H2
Taff Street (Pontypridd) **32** E2
Taff Street (Tongwynlais) ...**37** B3
Taff Street (Treherbert) **7** C5
Taff Terrace (Abercynon)...**26** F6
Taff Terrace (Blaen Clydach)
...............................**12** G2
Taff Terrace (Radyr) **37** C6
Taff Terrace (Treorchy) **8** F3
Taff Vale **26** H2
Taff Vale Centre **32** E2
Taff Vale Court **19** C6
Taff Vale Flats **32** E3
Taff Villas **33** B1/**34** F6
Taffs Fall Road **39** C5
Taffs Mead Road................**39** C5
Tafwys Walk **42** E4
Tai Bach **21** D6
Tai Cap Coch **6** F2
Tai Cwm **14** G4
Tai Cwm Cottages.............**14** E2
Tai Dyffryn **38** G2
Tai Ebenezer **27** C2
Tai Fforest Cottages **28** G6
Tai Gilfach*, Heol Gerrig **18** E2
Tai Mawr Road **18** G5
Tai Newydd (Pontypridd) ...**39** A2
Tai Newydd (Ynysybwl) **25** B5
Tai Penyard **19** C6
Tai Siriol **27** D6
Tai yn y Banwen **26** G1
Tai yr Efail **20** E1
Tai Ysgol Fach...................**18** E2
Tair Briallu **1** C2
Tair Eglwys **2** H3
Tair Heol **29** D3
Tair Twynau **20** F1
Talbot Close **35** C4
Talbot Road **35** B4/C4
Talbot Square (M. Tydfil) ...**19** C6
Talbot Square (Talbot Grn.)
...............................**35** B4
Taldwyn Terrace **22** G2
Taliesin **13** B2
Tallis Street **8** E4/F6
Talyfan Road......................**17** D5
Talygarn Close **17** A3
Talygarn Drive **17** A3
Tan y Bryn (Abertridwr) **40** F3
Tan y Bryn (Beddau) **33** C6
Tan y Bryn (Brynna) **17** A4
Tan y Bryn (Maerdy) **9** B2
Tan y Bryn (Mt. Ash) **23** D6

Tan y Bryn (Porth) **14** F5
Tan y Fron **8** F4
Tan y Marian **9** B3
Tan y Pych............................**7** A3
Tan yr Allt **35** D5
Tan yr Allt Villas*, Woodfield Ter.
...............................**23** D5
Tanyard Place **3** D5
Tanybryn Place **19** D4
Tanybryn Street **3** C4
Tanybryn Terrace (Pontygwaith)
...............................**12** E4
Tanybryn Villas **2** H4
Tanycoed Street **23** D5
Tanycoed Terrace **6** G3
Tavern y Coed **34** H2
Tawelfan (Nelson) **27** D5
Tawelfryn (M. Tydfil) **18** G3
Teamans Row **37** A4
Tegfan (Caerphilly) **41** C4
Tegfan (Maerdy) **9** C3
Tegfan (Pontyclun) **17** B2
Teify Terrace **10** F5
Telekebir Road **31** C1
Temperence Place..............**32** F2
Temple Street*, High St. **21** A1
Tenby Court........................**41** A3
Tennyson Close **39** A1
Tenth Avenue **19** D3
Terrace, The **36** H5
Terrys Way **17** C6
Third Avenue (Caerphilly) ..**41** C3
Third Avenue (M. Tydfil) **19** C3
Thirlmere Terrace **4** G4
Thistle Terrace...................**11** A6
Thomas Jones Square **22** G3
Thomas Place (Porth) **14** H4
Thomas Place (Ynyshir) **12** G5
Thomas Street (Aberdare)...**3** C2
Thomas Street (Aberfan)....**24** G2
Thomas Street (Abertridwr) **40** F5
Thomas Street (Caerphilly) **41** A2
Thomas Street (Gilfach Goch)
...............................**15** B5
Thomas Street (Maerdy) **9** A1
Thomas Street (Mt. Ash) ...**23** C5
Thomas Street (Nelson) **28** E6
Thomas Street (Pentre).......**9** A4
Thomas Street (Penygraig) **13** B3
Thomas Street (Pontypridd)
...............................**32** E2
Thomas Street (Tonypandy)
...............................**11** A6/**12** H2
Thomas Street (Treharris) ..**27** B3
Thomas Street (Trethomas)
...............................**43** B1
Thomas Terrace (Aberdare) **4** E6
Thomas Terrace*, Graig Terrace
...............................**20** E3
Thomasville **43** B3
Thompson Street (Pontypridd)
...............................**31** C1
Thompson Street (Trehafod)
...............................**29** C1
Thompson Villas **29** C1
Thorn Court **4** H6
Thornbury Close **18** F6
Thornhill Cottages **4** G6
Thornwood Place...............**27** B3
Three Oaks Close **42** F1
Three Salmon Street **21** A2
Thurston Road **32** F1
Thurston Street **26** G4

Timothy Place **4** F5
Tir Coed..............................**41** B2
Tir Mab Ellis Villas.............**33** C1
Tir Meibion Lane **35** C4
Tir y Graig **39** A5
Tirafon Court **17** B2
Tirbach Houses*, Tirfounder Rd.
...............................**4** G6
Tirfounder Road **4** G5/G6
Toghill Drive **38** H6
Tollgate Close **42** F2
Ton Hywel **14** F5
Ton Row **8** H6/**9** A5
Ton y Felin **39** A1
Ton y Felin Road **42** E4
Ton Coch Terrace **6** H1
Tonteg Close **39** A5
Tonteg Road **39** A5
Tonyrefail Bypass **13** D4
Tonyrefail Road (Beddau) ..**33** B1
Tonyrefail Road (Tonyrefail)
...............................**31** A6
Tor View.............................**42** F1
Tower Road **1** A2
Tower Street **32** F4
Towers, The..........................**1** A2
Towyn Way **39** A5
Trafalgar Terrace **9** C6/**11** A2
Tram Road*, Heol y Graig....**1** D5
Tramroad Lane **19** C5
Tramroad Terrace **21** A1
Tramroadside (Edwardsville)
...............................**26** H2
Tramroadside (Heolgerrig) **18** E1
Tramroadside (M. Tydfil) ...**18** G1
Tramroadside (Treharris)
...............................**27** A3/A5
Tramroadside North **19** C6
Tramroadside South **21** B2
Tramway **1** B2
Trap Lane **3** D3
Trap Well **42** G2
Tre Ifor **2** H2
Tre Telynog..........................**4** G5
Trealaw Road **11** B6
Treasure Street **8** F2
Trebanog Road **14** F6
Trebanog Terrace **1** B6
Treble Lock Cottages*,
    Cardiff Road **38** F3
Tredegar Avenue...............**17** D5
Tredegar Close **17** C4
Tredegar Flats*, Dranllwyn Lane
...............................**43** B5
Trefelin **2** H5/**3** A1
Treforest Court **32** G5
Tregarth Close....................**36** H5
Tregarth Court **36** H5
Tregwilym **4** G5
Trehafod Bypass **29** B4
Trehafod Road **29** C5
Treharne Court **14** G4
Treharne Flats **39** A2
Treharne Road **26** H1
Treharne Street (Cwmparc)..**8** F6
Treharne Street (Merthyr Vale)
...............................**24** G1
Treharne Street (Pentre) **8** H4
Treharne Terrace **26** G1
Trem y Castell **41** A6
Trem y Cwm **36** F1
Trem y Glyn **14** F5
Trem y Mynydd **7** B5

Tremle Court 8 F2
Trenant 1 C3
Treneol 5 C2
Trenos Gardens..............17 B6
Trenos Place 17 B6
Tressilian Place 26 F6
Trevelyan Court 42 F4
Trevethick Street 19 C6
Trevithick Gardens 21 B2
Trevor Close 20 F1
Trevor Street (Aberdare) 3 C4
Trevor Street (Treorchy) 8 F2
Trewaun.............................1 B3
Triangle, The (M. Tydfil) ...18 H4
Triangle, The (Mt. Ash) ...23 C2
Tridwr Road 40 F5
Trinity Road 13 B1
Trip Terrace 9 A4
Troed y Bryn 41 B2
Troed y Rhiw Road 23 C2
Troedpennar Terrace 26 G4
Troedrhiw Trwyn 31 B1
Troedyrhiw Road..............14 G2
Troedyrhiw Terrace...........8 G3
Tudor Avenue 1 A1
Tudor Close 24 H2
Tudor Court 9 A6
Tudor Gardens 43 B6
Tudor Mews 17 D1
Tudor Place 4 E5
Tudor Road 9 A6
Tudor Street (Ferndale) 10 F5
Tudor Street (M. Tydfil) 19 B6
Tudor Street (Rhydyfelin) ..32 H6
Tudor Terrace (Aberdare) 3 B2
Tudor Terrace (M. Tydfil)...19 B6
Tudor Way 33 A2/36 H1
Turberville Road 14 G2
Turberville Street 11 B3
Turberville Terrace 13 C2
Twelfth Avenue 19 D3
Twyn Bedw 14 G5
Twyn Carmel 18 F5/F6
Twyn Cottages................41 B4
Twyn Gwyn Road 13 D2
Twyn y Eos 7 D5
Twyn, The 42 E5
Twynygarreg 27 A2
Twynyrodyn Road 21 B1
Ty Abbeyfield....................7 C5
Ty Alban 11 A5
Ty Bethania 8 F2
Ty Bruce Road...................1 B1
Ty Bryn Seion*, North St. ...20 E4
Ty Bryncoch*, Bryn Coch....38 F5
Ty Bryngoleu....................24 G2
Ty Canol Lane (Machen)...43 B5
Ty Canol Lane (Trethomas)43 A1
Ty Capel 38 G6
Ty Capel Zion 12 E2
Ty Coch 43 D3
Ty Crwyn 34 G5
Ty Dawel 16 G3
Ty Dewi 9 A6
Ty Draw Place 4 E3
Ty Draw Road 3 D3
Ty Draw Terrace 7 A4
Ty Du Road 28 E6
Ty Ebenezer 12 E1
Ty Fry 9 A6
Ty Fry Villas*, Highland Pl. ..3 B4
Ty Glasfryn 12 E1
Ty Gwaunfarren................19 B2

Ty Gwyn Road (Church Village)
....34 G4
Ty Gwyn Road (Pontypridd)
....32 G2
Ty Heddlu 7 D5
Ty Isaf (Caerphilly) 41 B3
Ty Isaf (Llanharry) 15 A6
Ty Isaf Bungalows 41 B3
Ty Isaf Road 9 B6
Ty Llunfan 15 B3
Ty Llwyd Parc 27 B4
Ty Llwyd Terrace.............27 B4
Ty Mawr Road 37 D6
Ty Nant Bungalows 41 B3
Ty Nant Court 37 A2
Ty Nant Road (Morganstown)
....37 A2
Ty Nant Road (Radyr) 37 B5
Ty Newydd (Mt. Ash)........23 B1
Ty Newydd (Trethomas) ...43 D3
Ty Pica Close 43 C6
Ty Pontrhun 24 F2
Ty Rhiw 38 H5
Ty Twyn 34 F4
Ty'r Person 34 G4
Ty'r Waun 38 G1
Tydfil Close 27 D3
Tydfil House 8 H3
Tydfil Road 42 G1
Tydfil Terrace (10) (M. Tydfil)
....19 B5
Tydfil Terrace (Troedyrhiw)22 G2
Tydraw 34 G4
Tydraw Place 4 E3
Tyfica Crescent 32 E2
Tyfica Road 32 E2
Tygwyn Street 19 D5
Tyla Glas 41 C6
Tyla Gwyn 38 F2
Tylacelyn Road 13 B2
Tylacoch 15 A6/B6
Tylacoch Place 8 E2
Tylcha Fach 16 H6
Tylcha Fach Bungalows ...16 H6
Tylcha Fach Close............16 H6
Tylcha Fach Terrace 16 H6
Tylcha Ganol 16 G6
Tylcha Isaf 16 G6
Tylcha Wen Close 16 F5
Tylcha Wen Crescent 16 F5
Tylcha Wen Terrace 16 F5
Tyle Fforest 7 D5
Tyle Garw Terrace............17 A1
Tyler Hendy 17 C1
Tyllwyd Street 19 D5
Tylors Court*, East Road....12 E1
Tymawr Parc 31 C1
Tymawr Road 31 C1
Tymawr Terrace 31 C1
Tymawr Uchaf 31 C1
Tymynydd Close 37 B4
Tyn y Banwen Road 26 G1
Tyn y Berllan 14 G5
Tyn y Coedcae 7 D5
Tyn y Parc 40 F4
Tyn y Waun 9 C5/11 A2
Tyn y Waun Road 43 C5
Tyn y Wern 16 G6
Tyn y Wern Terrace...........43 A1
Tynant Road (Beddau) 33 C6
Tynant Road (Creigiau)....36 G6
Tynewydd Square............14 G2
Tyntaldwyn Road 22 G2

Tyntyla Avenue 9 D6/11 B2
Tyntyla Park.....................11 B3
Tyntyla Road.............9 D6/11 B3
Tyntyla Terrace 9 C6/11 A2
Tynybedw Close 8 H3
Tynybedw Street 8 G3
Tynybedw Terrace 8 G2
Tynybryn Road 16 F3
Tynycai Place 13 C3
Tynycoed Terrace 19 D5
Tynycoed Villas 10 E3
Tynycymmer Close 14 G3
Typica Cottages 31 C1
Tyrfelin Street 23 C5
Tyrheol 2 H4

U

Underhill Drive 39 A6
Underhill Villas...................3 D5
Underwood 42 E6
Underwood Terrace
(Abertridwr) 40 H5
Underwood Terrace
(Pontypridd) 31 C1
Union Place (M. Tydfil) 21 A1
Union Place (Tylorstown) ..11 H6
Union Street (Pontypridd)..32 E3
Union Street (Aberdare)
.............................2 H6/3 B1
Union Street (Ferndale) 10 F5
Union Street (Gelli) 9 B6
Union Street (M. Tydfil) 21 B1
Union Street (Mt. Ash) 23 B3
Union Terrace 21 B1
Unity Street 3 B4
Universal Court 40 E2
Universal Villas 40 E1
Uplands 9 B5
Uplands, The 37 B6
Upper Alma Place 8 H3
Upper Alma Terrace 32 F3
Upper Brynhyfryd Terrace ..40 F2
Upper Bwllfa Cottages.......9 A6
Upper Canning Street 8 H5
Upper Church Street 32 E2
Upper Colliers Row 18 G2
Upper Edward Street (7) ...19 B6
Upper Elizabeth Street 20 E4
Upper Forest Level 23 D3
Upper Francis Street 40 F5
Upper Gertrude Street......26 G5
Upper Glyn Gwyn Street ...43 B1
Upper Gynor Place 14 G1
Upper High Street (Bedlinog)
....28 G5
Upper High Street (Cefn Coed)
....18 G3
Upper Mount Pleasant 22 G3
Upper Regent Street 3 C4
Upper Row........................20 F3
Upper St. Albans Road 7 A3
Upper Taff Street 7 B5
Upper Terrace 12 E2
Upper Thomas Street 21 A1
Upper Union Street 20 F4
Upper Vaughan Street......31 D2
Upton Place.......................36 F1
Upton Street (Porth) 14 G2
Upton Street (Tonypandy) ..13 B2
Urban Street 19 D4
Usk Villas*, Cardiff Road....23 C3

V

Vale Gardens...................32 E1
Vale View (Llanharan) 17 C4
Vale View*, Abercynon Road
....26 F3
Vale View Street 13 C3
Vale View Terrace 23 C5
Valley View Street 5 D1
Van Road..........................42 E5
Van Terrace 42 G5
Vanfield Close 42 F5
Vaughan Street 31 D2
Vaughan Terrace (M. Tydfil)
....18 H4
Vaughan Terrace (Mt. Ash) 25 C1
Vaynor Lane 18 G3
Vaynor Road...........18 G3/19 A1
Vaynor Street 14 G2
Vaynors Villas 18 H3
Venture Court*, Greenway..42 F1
Vernon Close...................19 D6
Viaduct Road 37 A1
Viburnum Rise.................36 H2
Vicarage Close (Tonypandy)
....13 C2
Vicarage Close (Tonyrefail)16 H3
Vicarage Close (Ystrad)
.............................9 D6/11 A2
Vicarage Court 34 G3
Vicarage Road (Tonypandy)
....13 C2
Vicarage Road (Ynyshir)....14 G1
Vicarage Terrace 8 F6
Victor Street.....................23 B3
Victoria Buildings*, The Square
....22 G2
Victoria Mews 17 B1
Victoria Square..................3 C3
Victoria Street (Dowlais) ...20 F3
Victoria Street (M. Tydfil) ...21 A1
Victoria Street (Merthyr Vale)
....24 H1
Victoria Street (Mt. Ash) ...23 C4
Victoria Street (Ton Pentre)..9 A6
Victoria Street (Tonypandy)13 C1
Victoria Street (Treharris) ..27 B3
Victoria Street (Treherbert) ..7 B5
Victoria Street (Ystrad)
.............................9 C5/11 A2
Victoria Terrace (Treharris) 27 A4
Victoria Terrace (Wattstown)
....12 G4
Victory Avenue 14 G2
View, The.........................11 A5
Village Way 37 D3
Vincent Place...................19 B6
Violet Street.......................3 D4
Virginia Close 42 E3
Virginia Terrace 42 E3
Virginia View 42 E3
Vivian Street 11 D2
Volunteer Street 8 H4
Vulcan Buildings*, Vulcan Road
....19 B6
Vulcan Road 19 B6

W

Wakelin Close 34 G4
Walk, The (Aberdare) 3 D2
Walk, The (M. Tydfil) 19 C6
Walkers Terrace*, Penylan St.
....21 D6

Wallhead Road.....

Wallhead Road 21 C2
Walnut Close 17 D1
Walnut Tree Close...........37 A5
Walnut Way 19 C4
Walsh Street 25 D1
Walter Street (Abercynon)..26 G5
Walter Street (Blaenllechau)
......................10 F3
Walter Street (Dowlais) 20 E3
Walters Road................31 D4
Walters Terrace (Aberfan)..24 G2
Walters Terrace (M. Tydfil) 21 B2
Ware Road 41 B6
Warlow Street 21 B2
Warren Close 32 H6
Warren Drive 42 E6
Warren Terrace 27 D4
Washington Buildings 14 H3
Waterloo Place (Aberdare) ..3 B1
Waterloo Place (Trethomas)
......................43 D3
Waterloo Street..............4 G4
Waterloo Terrace Road 43 D3
Watford Close 41 D6
Watford Rise 41 D6
Watford Road 41 C6
Watkin Rhys Court...........13 B1
Waun Cottages 18 E2
Waun Erw 42 E2
Waun Fach Street 42 E3
Waun Ganol Street 42 E3
Waun Hir 34 F2
Waun Hir Cottages 34 F2
Waun Road 11 A6
Waun Row 2 H3
Waun Wen 14 F6
Waunbant Court.............18 F5
Waunfach Street Flats.......41 D3
Waunfain 41 C1
Waunllwyd 1 D3
Waunrhydd Road.............16 F3
Wayne Cottages 4 E6
Wayne Street (Aberdare)....3 B2
Wayne Street (Porth) 14 G2
Wayne Street (Trehafod)...29 C5
Weatherall Street............3 C3
Webster Street..............27 B2
Wedgewood Court 42 F4
Well Place 4 F4
Well Street (Abercynon)....26 F5
Well Street (Cefn Coed) 18 H4
Well Street (M. Tydfil) 19 B5
Wellfield...................33 C5
Wellfield Court..............34 G3
Wellfield Mews 33 C5
Wellington Street (Aberdare) 3 B1
Wellington Street (Tongwynlais)
......................37 B2
Wellingtonia Close...........19 B2
Wenallt Court................4 E2
Wenallt Road................4 D2
Wengraig Road.............13 C1
Werfa Close 4 E1
Werfa Lane 4 F1
Wern Caiach Cottages 28 E5
Wern Cottages 2 H4
Wern Crescent.............28 E5
Wern Ddu 42 G6
Wern Isaf 20 F3
Wern Lane.................18 G2
Wern Road (M. Tydfil) 18 H4
Wern Road (Tonypandy) ...13 B1
Wern Street (Clydach Vale) 12 F2

Wern Street (Dowlais) 20 F3
Wernddu Court................ 42 G5
Wernganol Houses 28 F6
Wesley Buildings 43 B5
Wesley Close (Dowlais)......20 E4
Wesley Close (Ystrad)
......................9 D5/11 A2
Wesley Cottages*, Church St.
......................24 E6
Wesley Cottages*, Wesley St.
......................26 G5
Wesley Hill.................43 B5
Wesley Place (Merthyr Vale)
......................24 H2
Wesley Place (Pentre).......9 A5
Wesley Road 41 B6
Wesley Street 26 G5
Wesley Villas*, Arfryn Terrace
......................12 E1
Wesleyan Cottages 29 C1
West Avenue 41 C4
West Grove 19 B5
West Mound Crescent.....39 A5
West Street (Abercynon)...26 G5
West Street (Pontypridd) ...32 F1
West Taff Street 14 H3
West View 38 H5
West View Crescent 27 D3
Westbourne Place (M. Tydfil)
......................21 B3
Westbourne Place (Troedyrhiw)
......................22 G3
Westbourne Terrace 17 B6
Westbury Houses 15 B3
Western Drive 41 B6
Western Street 29 C5/31 A1
Westfield Court 35 D5
Westfield Road 30 E4
Westhill Drive 35 D5
Weston Terrace.............13 D5
Weston Terrace (Cwmparc)..8 F6
Weston Terrace (Williamstown)
......................13 D5
Weston Terrace (Ynyshir)...12 G6
Westside Road 40 E2
Westview Terrace 42 G2
Westwood Drive 27 A3
Wheatley Place 21 C2
Wheatsheaf Lane 21 A1
Whitcombe Street 3 C3
White Cross Lane 41 B3
White Hart 43 A5
White Hart Cottages 43 A5
White Hart Drive 43 A5
White Rose Cottages.......36 E4
White Street (Caerphilly) 42 E5
White Street (Dowlais)........20 E3
Whitebeam Close 19 B2
Whitefield Street 8 H6
Whiterock Avenue 31 D1
Whiterock Close 31 D1
Whiterock Drive 31 D1
Whitting Street...............14 G1
Wilfried Way 15 C6
Wilkins Terrace 41 D1
William Harris Bungalows ..40 G5
William Street (Abercwmboi) 6 F2
William Street (Abercynon) 26 G5
William Street (Abertridwr)..40 F5
William Street (Brynna) 17 A1
William Street (Cilfynydd) ..30 H4
William Street (Llwynypia)...11 C4
William Street (M. Tydfil) 21 B2

William Street (8) (Morgantown)
......................19 B6
William Street (Treherbert) ..7 B4
William Street (Trethomas) 43 B1
William Street (Ynyshir).....12 H6
William Street (Ystrad).........9 B5
Williams Close..............39 C4
Williams Court 9 C5
Williams Place (M. Tydfil) ..19 D5
Williams Place (Porth).......14 G3
Williams Place (Rhydyfelin)
......................39 B4/C4
Williams Terrace (M. Tydfil)21 C1
Williams Terrace (Treharris)
......................27 B2
Williamstown 19 A6
Willow Close 36 E2
Willow Grove 3 A3
Willow Road (Llanharry) ...15 B6
Willow Road (M. Tydfil) 19 B3
Willow Street 39 A2
Willow Terrace (Mt. Ash)...23 D6
Willow Terrace (Troedyrhiw)
......................22 G2
Willowford Cottages...........38 E2
Willowford, The 38 E1
Willows, The (Aberdare) 3 A3
Willows, The (Trethomas) ..43 A1
Wilson Place 9 A2
Wimborne Street 20 E3
Winch Fawr Park 18 E2
Winch Fawr Road.........18 E1/F6
Wind Street (Aberdare) ..3 C3/C4
Wind Street (Blaenllechau) 10 F4
Wind Street (Ynyshir) 14 G1
Windermere Close 4 F4
Windsor Avenue 37 A5
Windsor Close 37 A5
Windsor Cottages 25 C6
Windsor Court (Pontyclun) 17 B1
Windsor Court (Radyr).......37 A5
Windsor Court (Ynysybwl)..25 C6
Windsor Crescent 37 B6
Windsor Drive 17 D1
Windsor Gardens 33 D5
Windsor Grove.............37 A5
Windsor Place (Abertridwr) 40 E5
Windsor Place (Dowlais) 20 F2
Windsor Place (M. Tydfil) ..19 C6
Windsor Place (Merthyr Vale)
......................24 H1
Windsor Place (Pentre).......8 H4
Windsor Place (Senghenydd)
......................40 F3
Windsor Place (Treharris) ..27 A3
Windsor Place (Ynysybwl)..25 C6
Windsor Road (Mt. Ash) ...23 C5
Windsor Road (Radyr).......37 B6
Windsor Road (Treforest) ..32 G4
Windsor Road (Treharris) ..26 H2
Windsor Street (Aberdare)
......................2 H5/3 A1
Windsor Street (Caerphilly) 42 E5
Windsor Street (Pentre).......8 H4
Windsor Street (Treherbert)..7 B5
Windsor Street (Treorchy) 8 F2
Windsor Street (Troedyrhiw)
......................22 F3
Windsor Terrace (Aberdare) 4 E2
Windsor Terrace (M. Tydfil)
......................21 B1
Windsor Villas 4 E2
Wingfield Avenue 33 C6

Wingfield Close 32 G2
Wingfield Rise 27 B4
Wingfield Street.............24 G1
Wingfield Terrace 27 B4
Winifred Street (Dowlais)....20 E3
Winifred Street (Mt. Ash)....23 D6
Winslade Avenue 16 G2
Witherdene Road............12 E3
Witts End 17 C6
Wood Road (Abercynon)...26 G5
Wood Road (Pontypridd) ...32 F3
Wood Street (Cilfynydd) 30 H5
Wood Street (Ferndale)......10 E4
Wood Street (Gilfach Goch)
......................15 A5
Wood Street (Maerdy) 9 A1
Wood Villas*, Main Road....25 D1
Woodfield Buildings*,
   Woodfield Terrace 14 H2
Woodfield Road 35 A4
Woodfield Street 17 B6
Woodfield Terrace (Mt. Ash)
......................23 D5
Woodfield Terrace (Porth)..14 H2
Woodfield Terrace (Trehafod)
......................29 B5
Woodland Crescent (Abercynon)
......................26 H4
Woodland Crescent (Treharris)
......................27 A4
Woodland Cottages.........28 H6
Woodland Court 26 G5
Woodland Crescent (Creigiau)
......................36 H5
Woodland Drive.............24 G2
Woodland Park 1 A6
Woodland Place (Bedlinog)
......................28 H6
Woodland Place (M. Tydfil) 21 B1
Woodland Place (Pontypridd)
......................31 D4
Woodland Road (Beddau)
......................33 D6/36 G1
Woodland Road (Mt. Ash) ..23 B2
Woodland Road (Tylorstown)
......................11 D3
Woodland Street 23 B2
Woodland Terrace (Aberdare)
......................5 D1
Woodland Terrace (Abertridwr)
......................40 F5
Woodland Terrace (M. Tydfil)
......................21 B1
Woodland Terrace (Mt. Ash)
......................23 B3
Woodland Terrace (Pontypridd)
......................31 D3
Woodland Terrace (Senghenydd)
......................40 F3
Woodland Terrace (Treorchy)
......................8 E1
Woodland Terrace*, Ash Grove
......................17 A1
Woodland Vale 8 F1
Woodland View 34 F5
Woodland Villas 27 A4
Woodland Way 27 A4
Woodlands (Llan. Fardre)
......................33 A1/D6
Woodlands (Taff's Well).....38 F6
Woodlands*, Henry Richard St.
......................22 H1
Woodlands Avenue 27 A3

Woodside Bungalows*, John St.
.............................23 D4
Woodview 17 A5
Woodville Place.................10 E4
Worcester Close 18 E2
Wordsworth Gardens 39 A1
Wordsworth Street...............5 B3
Wrgant Place......................9 A1
Wyndham Court...................4 F6
Wyndham Crescent.............4 F6
Wyndham Street (Brynna)..17 B6
Wyndham Street (Dowlais) 20 E4
Wyndham Street (Gilfach Goch)
.............................15 A2
Wyndham Street (Machen) 43 C5
Wyndham Street (Pentre) ...9 A6
Wyndham Street (Porth) ...14 H4
Wyndham Street (Tongwynlais)
.............................37 B2
Wyndham Street (Tonypandy)
.............................13 B2
Wyndham Street (Treherbert)
.............................7 B4
Wyndham Street (Troedyrhiw)
.............................22 G3

Y

Y Cilgant 41 C1
Y Deri 33 B2/34 F6
Y Dolydd 41 C6
Y Felin Ffrwd 41 C3
Y Garth 2 F5
Y Graig 20 E1
Y Parc 36 F6
Y Waun 25 B6
Yew Close 19 C3
Yew Street (M. Tydfil) 21 A2
Yew Street (Taff's Well)....38 F5
Yew Street (Troedyrhiw) ...22 G3
Ynys Close 32 H5
Ynys Hir 30 F3
Ynys Las 27 D5
Ynys Park Terrace.............9 A5
Ynys Street 12 H5
Ynys Terrace..................32 H5
Ynys Wen 10 F5
Ynysangharad Road 32 F2
Ynysbryn Close 35 C4
Ynyscorrwg Road 39 A3
Ynyscynon Road 11 B6
Ynyscynon Street 4 F4
Ynyscynon Terrace 4 F4
Ynysddu 17 A1/35 A6
Ynysfach Estate 18 G2/21 A2
Ynysfach Road 18 G2
Ynysfach Yard 37 B2
Ynysfeio Avenue 7 D6
Ynysfeio Close 7 D6
Ynysgau Street 9 B6
Ynysgored Cottages 22 G4
Ynysgyfeilion Road 32 E1
Ynyshir Road 12 G4/14 G1
Ynysllwyd Road.................4 E5
Ynysllwyd Street 3 C4
Ynyslyn Road 39 B3
Ynysmaerdy Terrace 35 A1
Ynysmeurig Road 26 G5
Ynysowen Fach 22 G6
'Ynystaf*, Cardiff Road.......24 H2
Ynyswen Road 8 E1
'Ynysybwl Road 29 D3
Ynysygored Road 22 G6
York Close 18 E1

York Court 37 A5
York Drive 33 B2
York Street (Aberdare) 5 D1
York Street (Mt. Ash).........23 C4
York Street (Porth) 14 H3
York Terrace*, Thomas St. 23 C5
Yr Aelwyn Flats 29 C2
Yr Allt 35 C3
Yr Graig 35 C4
Yr Hen Lawnt....................13 B3
Yr Hen Ysgol 3 B2
Yr Hendre 38 G1
Ysgubor Fach 43 B5
Ystrad Road.......................9 A5
Ystrad Terrace....................9 B6
Ystradbarwig Terrace 36 H1
Ystradfechan House 8 F3

Z

Zion Court 33 C6
Zion Terrace 11 A6
Zoar Terrace 27 A4

HOSPITALS

Aberdare General Hospital ..3 D2
Caerphilly District Hospital 41 C6
Dewi Sant Hospital 32 E3
Llwynypia General Hospital11 C3
Mardy Hospital 21 C3
Mountain Ash General Hosp.
.............................23 B1
Pontypridd and District Hosp.
.............................32 G2
Prince Charles Hospital 19 B3
Royal Glamorgan Hospital..35 A2
St. Tydfils Hospital............21 B1
Whitchurch Psychiatric Hosp.
.............................37 D6
Ysbyty George Thomas 8 G4

POLICE STATIONS

Abercynon Police Station ..26 G5
Aberdare Police Station........3 C4
Bedwas Police Station 42 G1
Caerphilly Police Station ...42 E6
Dowlais Police Station.......20 E3
Gurnos Police Station 19 B2
Hirwaun Police Station 1 A2
Llantrisant Police Station 35 B4
Merthyr Tydfil Police Station
.............................21 A1
Mountain Ash Police Station
.............................23 B3
Pontypridd Police Station .32 E2
Porth Police Station..........14 H3
Ton Pentre Police Station 8 H5
Tonypandy Police Station .13 B1
Tonyrefail Police Station ...16 F4
Trecynon Police Station 2 H5
Treharris Police Station 27 B3

TOURIST INFORMATION OFFICES

Caerphilly TIC
Tel. 02920 880011 ......42 E5
Merthyr Tydfil TIC
Tel. 01685 379884 ......21 A1

SCHOOLS & COLLEGES

Abercanaid Community School
.............................21 C6
Abercerdin Prim. School 15 A3
Abercynon Infants School ..26 G5
Aberdare Boys Comp. Schoool
.............................2 G6/3 A1
Aberdare Girls Comp. Sch. ..3 D3
Aberdare Town Prim.Sch. 3 D4
Aberllechau Prim. School ..12 G4
Abernant Primary School......4 E2
Abertaf Primary School 26 G4
Afon Taf High School 22 G3
Alaw Primary School 13 D1
Bedlinog Primary School ...28 G5
Bedwas High School 42 H1
Bedwas Infants School 42 G1
Bedwas Junior School.......42 G1
Bishop Hedley R. C. High School
.............................19 D5
Blaengwawr Comp. School ..3 D5
Blaengwawr Prim. School 3 D5
Bodringallt Primary School ..9 C5
Brecon Road Infs. School ..19 B6
Bryn Deri Primary School ..37 A5
Bryncelynnog Comp. Sch...33 C5
Brynnau Primary School 17 A5
Caedraw Primary School ...21 A2
Caegarw Primary School ..23 C2
Capcoch Primary School 6 F2
Caradog Primary School 3 C3
Cardinal Newman R.C. Comp.
School 39 B2
Carnetown Primary Sch. 26 F5
Cefn Primary School 30 E4
Cilfynydd Primary School ..30 H4
Coedpenmaen Primary School
.............................32 F1
Coedylan Comp. School ...30 G3
Coedylan Prim. School 32 E1
Coleg Morgannwg
(Nantgarw Campus) 38 F1
Coleg Morgannwg
(Pontypridd Campus)
.....................32 H6/39 A2
Coleg Morgannwg
(Aberdare Campus)
.....................2 G5/3 A1
Coleg Morgannwg
(Rhondda Campus) 11 B3
Coleg Morgannwg (GCADT)
.............................32 H3
Comin Infants School 3 B2
Comin Junior School....2 H6/3 B2
Coryton Primary School 37 D5
Craig yr Hesg Prim. Sch....30 G4
Creigiau Primary School 36 H5
Cwm Golau Intergrated
Childrens Centre 21 D6
Cwm Ifor Prim. School.......41 B2
Cwmaber Infants School ...40 G4
Cwmaber Junior School ...40 G5
Cwmaman Infants School 5 C3
Cwmbach Infants School 4 G5
Cwmbach Junior School 4 G4
Cwmbach Nursery School ...4 G5
Cwmbach Primary School....4 G5
Cwmclydach Prim. School 12 G2
Cwmdar Primary School 2 F6
Cwmlai Primary School 16 G6

Cyfarthfa High School.........21B1
Cyfarthfa High School (Lower)
.............................19 A5
Cyfarthfa Junior School 19 A5
Cymmer Infants School.......14 G4
Cymmer Junior School 14 G4
Darran Park Prim. School ..10 F4
Darranlas Prim School........23 B4
Dinas Junior School 13 C2
Dolau Primary School 17 B6
Dowlais Infants School 20 F4
Edwardsville Prim. School..26 H1
Ferndale Community Sch.....9 C2
Ferndale Infants School.....10 F4
Ffynnon Taff Prim. School..38 F5
Gelli Primary School 9 B5
Gellifaelog Prim. School 20 E3
Gilfach Goch Infs. School ..15 B1
Glanffrwd Infants School ...25 B5
Glantaf Infants School 32 H5
Glenboi Primary School........6 H4
Glynhafod Junior School 5 A3
Goetre Infants School 19 B4
Goetre Junior School.........19 B4
Graig-y-Rhacca Primary School
.............................43 C1
Graig-y-Wion Prim. Sch. ...32 E3
Greenfield Special School...21 D6
Greenhill Primary School....28 H2
Gurnos Nursery School 19 B4
Gwaelod-y-Garth Prim. School
.............................38 F5
Gwauncelyn Prim. School ..34 H4
Gwaunfarren Prim. Sch. ...19 C5
Gwaunmeisgyn Primary School
.............................36 F1
Gwernllyn Junior School ...20 G3
Hafod Primary School 29 B5
Hawthorn High School.......39 A3
Hawthorn Prim. School 39 A3
Hendre Infants School 41 B3
Hendre Junior School 41 B4
Hendredenny Park Prim. School
.............................41 A4
Hendreforgan Prim. Sch. ...15 B5
Heol y Celyn Prim. School.39 A2
Heolgerrig School 18 E2
Hirwaun Primary School 1 B3
Lansbury Park Infs. & Jun. Schs.
.............................42 G3
Llancaeach Junior School ..28 E6
Llanfabon Infants School...27 D6
Llanharan Primary School...17 D4
Llanhari Primary School 15 A6
Llanilltud Faerdref Prim. School
.............................34 H4
Llantrisant Prim. Sch. 35 C2
Llwydcoed Primary Sch.......2 H3
Llwyncelyn Infs. School 29 A4
Llwyncrwn Prim. School 36 E1
Llwynypia Primary School ..11 A6
Machen Primary School 43 C5
Maerdy Infants School 9 A2
Maerdy Junior School 9 B2
Maes-y-Bryn Primary School
.....................33 B1/34 F6
Maesgwyn Special School....2 F5
Maesycoed Prim. School....31 D3
Merthyr Tydfil College
.....................18 G2/21 A1
Miskin Primary School........23 C5
Mount Pleasant Primary School
.............................24 H4

Mountain Ash Comp. Sch......

Mountain Ash Comp. Sch...**23** A1
Nant y Parc Prim. School ..**40** E2
Nantgarw Infants School **38** F2
Newtown Primary School ...**23** D4
Oaklands Primary School ...**6** E1
Our Lady's R.C. Primary School
......**23** C4
Pantysgallog Prim. School..**20** F2
Parc Lewis Primary Sch....**32** G3
Parc Primary School **8** E4
Park Lane Special School
...............**2** G6/3 A2
Pen y Dre High School **19** C3
Penderyn Primary School ...**1** B5
Pengeulan Prim. School **23** D5
Penpych Primary School......**7** A3
Penrhiw-fer Infs. School ...**13** D6
Penrhiwceiber Prim. Sch. ..**23** D6
Penrhys Primary School **11** D2
Pentre Primary School **8** H3
Penygraig Infants School ..**13** C2
Penygraig Junior School ...**13** B2
Penygwasi Prim. School ...**35** C4
Penyrenglyn Prim. School....**7** D6
Penywaun Primary School ..**2** E3
Perthcelyn Prim. School ...**23** D6
Plasyfelin Prim. School **41** D3
Pontrhondda Prim. School..**11** B3
Pontyclun Primary School ..**17** B2
Pontygwaith Prim. School ..**11** D4
Porth Community School **14** F2
Porth Infants School **14** H2
Porth Junior School **14** H3
Radyr Primary School **37** A5
Rhigos Primary School **1** D5
Rhiwgarn Infants School ...**14** F6
Rhydfelin Nursery School ..**39** A2
Robertstown Nursery Sch. ..**3** C1
SS. Gabriel & Raphael R.C.
 Prim. School..............**13** B1
St. Aloysius R.C. Prim. School
...............**19** B4
St. Cenydd School..............**41** B4
St. Helen's Catholic Prim. School
...............**42** G4
St. Illtyd's R.C. Primary School
...............**20** E4
St. John the Baptist School ..**3** B3
St. Margarets R.C. Prim. School
...............**3** B4
St. Martins Comp. School ..**42** E6
St. Mary's R.C. Prim. Sch...**21** A2
St. Michaels Prim. School ..**32** G5
Talbot Green Special
 Needs Centre.............**35** B4
Ton Infants School...............**9** A5
Ton Pentre Junior School **8** H5
Tongwynlais Prim. School...**37** C3
Tonypandy Community
 College **13** B2
Tonypandy Prim. School ...**13** B1
Tonyrefail Nursery School..**16** G3
Tonyrefail Primary School..**16** G3
Tonyrefail School.................**16** E4
Tonysguboriau Prim. Sch. ..**35** A5
Trallwng Infants School **32** F1
Trealaw Primary School **13** C1
Tref-y-Rhyg Prim. School ..**16** H3
Trefechan Nursery School..**19** A2
Treforest Primary School ..**32** F4
Treharris Nursery School....**27** B3
Trehopcyn Primary School **31** C1
Trelewis Primary School **27** C2

Treorchy Comp. School........**8** F3
Treorchy Primary School......**8** G2
Trerobart Primary School ..**29** C1
Troedyrhiw Infants School..**22** G2
Troedyrhiw Junior School ..**22** G2
Twyn School, The **42** E5
Twynrodyn Community School
.... **21** C1/C2
Tylorstown Prim. School **12** E1
Tynywern Prim. School **43** A2
Williamstown Prim. Sch. **13** D4
Y Pant Comp. School **35** B6
Ynysboeth Infants School..**26** E1
Ynysboeth Junior School ..**26** E1
Ynyscynon Early Years Centre
.....................**11** D4
Ynyshir Primary School......**14** H1
Ynysowen Prim. School **24** G2
Ynyswen Infants School **8** E1
Ysgol Gyfun Cymer Rhondda
.......................**14** G4
Ysgol Gyfun Garth Olwg ...**34** G4
Ysgol Gyfun Llanhari **15** A6
Ysgol Gyfun Rhydywaun **1** D3
Ysgol Gymraeg Rhyd y Grug
........................**27** A4
Ysgol Gynradd Coed y Dderwen
......................**18** H5
Ysgol Gynradd Gymraeg
 Abercynon **26** G4
Ysgol Gynradd Gymraeg
 Aberdar **2** G6/3 A2
Ysgol Gynradd Gymraeg
 Bodringallt **9** C5
Ysgol Gynradd Gymraeg
 Bronllwyn **9** C5
Ysgol Gynradd Gymraeg Caerffili
.......................**42** E3
Ysgol Gynradd Gymraeg
 Castellau **33** B6
Ysgol Gynradd Gymraeg
 Evan James **31** D2
Ysgol Gynradd Gymraeg
 Garth Olwg.................**34** G4
Ysgol Gynradd Gymraeg
 Gymuned Llantrisant ..**17** C1
Ysgol Gynradd Gymraeg
 Llwyncelyn **29** A4
Ysgol Gynradd Gymraeg
 Llyn y Forwyn **10** F5
Ysgol Gynradd Gymraeg
 Pont Sion Norton **30** G6
Ysgol Gynradd Gymraeg
 Tonyrefail **16** G3
Ysgol Gynradd Gymraeg
 Ynyswen **8** E1
Ysgol Hen Felin...............**9** D6
Ysgol Ifor Bach **40** F1
Ysgol Santes Tudful **19** D6
Ysgol Ty Coch **39** A6
Ysgol y Graig Primary. **18** H3
Ysgol yr Eos **13** C2

INDUSTRIAL ESTATES

Aberaman Enterprise Park ..**4** G6
Aberaman Park Industrial Estate
..................**4** F6/6 F1
Aberdare Business Park **3** C1
Abergorki Industrial Estate ..**8** E2
Albion Industrial Estate **30** G3
Bartlett Street Ind. Estate....**42** F5
Bedwas House Ind. Estate **42** E1
Bryncae Industrial Estate ..**17** C6
Bryngelli Industrial Estate ...**1** A2
Caerphilly Business Park....**42** F5
Cambrian Ind. Est. East Side*,
 Coedcae Lane **35** A6
Cambrian Ind. Est. West Side*,
 Coedcae Lane **35** A6
Cambrian Ind. Estate..........**35** A6
Cambrian Industrial Park....**12** G2
Coedcae Lane Ind. Estate ..**35** A6
Crossways Retail Park........**42** F1
Cwm Cynon Bus. Park **23** D4
Cyfarthfa Retail Park
........................**18** G1/**19** A6
Cyfarthfa Industrial Estate ..**19** A5
Cymmer Road Ind. Estate ..**14** G2
Dinas Enterprise Centre **14** G2
Dinas Isaf Ind. Estate (East)
........................**13** D5
Dinas Isaf Ind. Estate (West)
........................**13** D6
Dowlais Industrial Estate ...**20** F5
Dr. William Price Bus. Centre
........................**32** G5
Dragon Park Ind. Estate ...**22** F4
E.F.I. Industrial Estate **19** A6
Ely Industrial Estate...........**13** C4
Ely Meadow Bus. Park **35** B3
Ely Valley Business Park (East)
........................**17** A1
Ely Valley Industrial Estate **17** A1
Enterprise Centre **22** E1
Fairfield Industrial Estate....**37** A1
Ferndale Industrial Estate ...**9** D3
Ffrwd Amos Ind. Estate **13** C2
Forest Farm Ind. Estate **37** B5
Garth Works Estate............**38** G6
Gelli Industrial Estate............**9** B5
Gelligron Industrial Estate ..**16** F2
Gellihirion Ind. Estate **39** C3
Glamorgan Ind. Estate........**11** B5
Glamorgan Vale Retail Park
........................**35** C5
Goat Mill Road Ind. Estate..**20** E5
Greenway Workshops........**42** G1
Gwaelod y Garth Ind. Estate
........................**37** A1
Harold Wilson Ind. Estate ..**42** G6
Highfield Industrial Estate ...**9** D3
Junction Industrial Centre ..**17** A1
Lanelay Industrial Estate ...**35** A6
Linde Industrial Park **22** F1
Llantrisant Business Park ..**35** B1
Llwyncelyn Ind. Estate.......**29** A4
Llwynypia Ind. Estate.........**11** B5
Maerdy Road Ind. Estate....**9** C3
Maesgwynne Ind. Estate ...**18** H5
Maritime Industrial Estate ..**31** D4
Merthyr Tydfil Industrial Park
........................**22** F2/H6
Midway Park **39** D3

Moy Road Ind. Estate **38** G6
Navigation Park..................**26** G5
Newpark Shopping Centre **35** C5
Newtown Industrial Estate
........................**33** B1/**34** G6
Oaklands Business Park **10** G5
Old Parish Road Industrial Estate
........................**29** D2
Pant Glas Industrial Estate
........................**42** H2/**43** A2
Pant Industrial Estate
........................**19** C2/D2/**20** E2
Parc Nantgarw **38** F1
Pavilion Industrial Estate **23** C3
Pengarnddu Bus. Park **20** H2
Pentrebach Ind. Estate **21** D5
Penygraig Ind. Estate **13** C2
Pontcynon Ind. Estate **26** F3
Pontygwaith Ind. Estate ...**12** F4
Pontygwindy Ind. Estate ...**41** D1
QED Centre......................**39** D5
Rheola Industrial Estate **14** H2
Riverside Industrial Park ...**39** C5
Robertstown Ind. Estate **3** C2
Standard Industrial Estate..**12** G5
Taff Business Centre **39** B4
The Beeches Ind. Estate **35** A6
Tonypandy Ent. Centre **11** B5
Tonypandy Ind. Estate........**11** B5
Trecynedd Ind. Estate **41** D2
Treforest Industrial Estate
........................**38** E1/**39** D6
Treherbert Industrial Estate..**7** C5
Treorchy Industrial Estate **8** G4
Triangle Business Park **21** C5
Ty Draw Industrial Estate **7** A5
Upper Boat Ind. Park..........**39** D5
Valley Innovation Centre....**26** G6
Venosa Trading Estate **42** F3
Wattstown Ind. Estate **12** G4
Woodlands Workshop Centre
........................**17** A1/**35** A6
Woodstock Business Park..**37** D3
Ynysboeth Factory Estate ..**26** E2
Ynyshir Industrial Estate ...**14** H1
Ynyswen Industrial Estate **8** E1